Hedgerow Harvest

Hedgerow Harvest

AMORET SCOTT

CONSERVES · CHUTNEYS · JAMS · JELLIES
PICKLES · PRESERVES · RELISHES · WINES · CHEESES
SOUPS AND SURPRISES

The Oxford Illustrated Press

Typeset by Oxprint Ltd, Oxford
Printed and bound in the UK by
Billing & Sons Ltd, Guildford and Worcester
for
Oxford Illustrated Press Ltd
Shelley Close, Headington,
Oxford OX3 8HB

This book is set in 11 on 13 pt Plantin

ISBN 0 902280 70 8

CONTENTS

HARVESTING

February	March	April	May	June
Sorrel	*Sorrel*	*Nettles*	*Nettles*	*Mint*
	Primroses	*Mint*	*Dandelions*	*Green walnuts*
		Dandelions	*Hawthorn flowers*	*Elderflowers*
			Mint	*Thyme flowers*
				Dandelions

CALENDAR

July	August	September	October
Elderflowers	*Bilberries*	*Apples*	*Nuts*
Bilberries	*Rowanberries*	*Blackberries*	*Apples*
Wild	*Mushrooms*	*Rowanberries*	*Damsons*
strawberries	*Raspberries*	*Elderberries*	*Rosehips*
Raspberries	*Blackberries*	*Mushrooms*	*Rowanberries*
		Rosehips	*Elderberries*
		Nuts	

November

Bullace

Apples

Sloes

THE HEDGEROW

The country hedge is one of the loveliest features of the English landscape giving it character and pattern. Like the countryside in general, hedgerows have been taken for granted until recently when the increasing interest in conservation and concern over intensive large-scale farming have drawn attention to a fast-diminishing asset. Many contain and conceal important historical evidence and most can still provide the ingredients for recipes which generations of countrymen have enjoyed.

Some of the hedges planted a thousand years ago are still in place performing their original function; they were the first cheap and effective way of marking property and safeguarding stock. The species chosen would be those at hand which were seen to be quick growing and, preferably, thorny. When the boundary was intended as a defence against marauders, additional strength was gained by digging a ditch and planting the trees on the resulting mound. The roots grew and bound the soil underneath to create the formidable roadside bank known in the West Country as a

'Devon hedge'. With no hard surface on the road, the tracks have gradually eroded leaving us the sunken lanes which offer a micro-climate to delight botanists and naturalists. A close study of an ordnance survey map may reveal short stretches of these lanes in many parts of the country. Some run parallel to a modern road, others survive as a forgotten link between two routes and look to a casual observer like a single overgrown hedge.

In 1971 a conference of historians and botanists was held at which papers were read on the possible dating of hedgerows by the number of species found in them. At the time a few scattered experiments had been conducted and the results indicated that the theory was worth further investigation. Such an attractive idea appealed immediately and since then many schools and local societies throughout the country have been involved in counting species and, where possible, relating the results to dated maps and charts. In spite of the many factors which have to be taken into account, a definite overall pattern is emerging. It is a fascinating exercise but it is also work of considerable urgency: experts have calculated that in some areas as much as seventy per cent of hedgerows have been lost in the past decade alone.

For a quick assessment of the age of your nearest hedge, stake out a 28-metre (30-yard) length and count the number of trees and shrubby species in it. It has been found that a reckoning of one species per century indicates the approximate age of the hedge. Your investigations can be checked against a dated feature such as a Roman road, drovers' route or a pilgrim way; there are few parts of the country which are far from one of these ancient green roads.

A hedgerow offers interest at all times of the year. In winter when there are no fruits to harvest, the bare branches sometimes disclose that a farmer has patched a gap with antiquated machinery, probably from the heavy horse era. There could also be a glimpse of stone: the Romans were the first to use inscribed blocks of stone to indicate the distance between points and a surprising number survive along their more remote routes. On certain roads decorative cast iron posts can be found. These were set up in the early nineteenth century to show, by a rebus and an arabic figure, the mileage to Bow Bells. The most commonly seen milestones are the shaped blocks of stone with the number of miles given to the nearest towns. Although some of these will have been erected comparatively recently, all milestones are now rightly considered as bygones worthy of preservation and local historians are cleaning them and recording their positions.

In addition to lost milestones, an overgrown hedge can hide and cover the rubbish of generations. Ditching on farms often produces a wide variety of interesting relics. Stoneware bottles with the names of local breweries and pubs impressed or printed upon them and glass lemonade bottles complete with their marble stopper are frequent survivors from some hot summer of seventy or so years ago. Bare branches expose strange tools which appear to have been carefully placed in the hedge by a long dead craftsman who had every intention of returning for them. Museum help will probably be necessary to identify tools from once common crafts such as flint knapping or thatching.

For country people the hedgerow was a source of medicine, food, drink, fuel, shelter and protection. It is hardly surprising that they endowed with spirits many of the most important plants growing in it. With the confident superiority of twentieth century knowledge we smile at some of the primitive associations. It now seems absurd for the shepherd to consider that the picking of lambs tails, or hazel catkins, might lead to losses among his flock. When medicine and botany were one science, the popular Doctrine of Signatures appeared very logical. Exponents of it in the seventeenth century argued that nature gave very clear indication by the appearance of plants and their manner of growth which plants were to be used for specific ailments. The walnut as a medicine for head complaints was cited as a particularly good example; its outer shell was a clear representation of the human skull concealing the convoluted inner kernel with its resemblance to the brain. By the same argument Dandelion Wine and the products of other yellow flowers were a certain cure for jaundice. The reasoning was carried to the splended conclusion that some plants were deliberately left without signatures in order to give a rarity value to the others.

It is now recognized that it might be unwise to dismiss out of hand all these long held theories. The Chelsea Physick Garden was founded in 1673 by the Worshipful Company of Apothecaries to grow and study medicinal herbs. Three hundred years later it is still supplying some of the leading hospitals in the world with plants which provide vital and irreplaceable ingredients for modern medicine.

The hedgerow is interpreted here as it is now found, containing a mixture of trees and plants, some of which have escaped from cultivation. Many of the recipes which follow originated in the nineteenth century or earlier when economics and the housewife's pride ensured that locally available foods were used to their best advantage. The simplicity of the recipes and their often modest ingredients mean that detail is all important for the best results. It is essential for success that the herbs, fruit and flowers are picked on a fine warm day and that any spices used be freshly ground. To do justice to recipes using delicately flavoured ingredients, butter should be used.

The chosen selection of possible fruits and flowers are those that have proved most delicious, are easy for everyone to identify and have a wide distribution; the fact that they are free is a bonus.

Hawtho
Liqueu

Mint
Jelly

Crystallized
Violets

FLOWERS AND HERBS

Dandelions, nettles and mint can be found growing prolifically throughout Britain and they have been as long and firmly established in the herbals as they have in the hedgerows. Their very omnipresence perhaps is responsible for their recommendation as cure-alls in the past and our indifference to them today.

Most children will identify 'fairy clocks', 'clocks and watches' or 'what o'clock', but their parents are unlikely to associate 'pee-a-bed' or 'wet-a-bed' with the ubiquitous dandelion. It is mainly the root and milky juice from the stem which have been used medically as a laxative and a mild diuretic; using the heads, the highly recommended recipe for Dandelion Wine which follows gives only a pleasant after effect.

The less conspicuous sorrel is also universally found and, like mint, enjoys a damp situation to grow in. Its country names of 'green sauce', 'gipsy's baccy' and 'sour sauce' indicate some of its uses. The sharp astringency of the young leaf was appreciated by the cook in the days before lemons were generally available. Sorrel has the added virtue in being one of the earliest plants in the year to put out its leaves.

Although it does not merit a recipe to itself, thyme is included in many of them as a valued aromatic ingredient. It is found creeping through the grass on dry sunny banks and is easiest to locate in mid-summer when it is in flower. It has a number of associations with death and is reported to scent the air forever where a murder has been committed. Its main importance, however, is in providing the favourite playground for fairies. Shakespeare was making use of common knowledge when he gave Queen Titania a bank of wild thyme as her throne. A seventeenth century recipe lists it as one of the principal ingredients in the potion which allows mortals a sight of the spirits. The less ambitious could put a sprig of thyme under their pillow in order to dream of their future husband.

It can only be the irritating prickly sting which makes the nettle unwelcome, because its many virtues as food, in medicine and as an alternative to flax, ensured it a large place in all herbals. Young nettles are easy to digest and there is a long tradition of using the leaves as a potherb. Country people still consider that its major value is as a blood purifier and tonic to the system after the sluggish winter months. In Scotland, in order to outwit the weather, plants would be forced under glass cloches to provide 'early spring kail'. A minimum of three meals which included nettles was considered necessary each spring to put one in good shape.

Nettles are only worth using in the kitchen when they are young, and not more than 18 cm high. After that, although the stems become too stringy for eating, they can be used for making cloth. The fibres are sufficiently versatile to be made into items ranging from sheets and tablecloths to fishing nets. If nettles persist in being a problem in your own hedgerow, in spite of cropping them to enjoy these recipes, be reassured by the Royal Horticultural Society who maintain that if they are cut down three times in three consecutive years, they will actually disappear.

Towards the middle of May the countryside is transformed by clouds of white blossom from elder and hawthorn. These trees hold a reputation for protective magic which is recognized in many parts of the Continent as well as in Britain. The month of May, which also gives its name to hawthorn, is dedicated to the pagan White Goddess, a being with many manifestations whose influence persists into the twentieth century. Branches from her sacred trees were gathered and used only for her feast day, 1st May; until the calendar was altered by eleven days in 1752, the trees were usually in bloom for the occasion. It was a time for celebrating fertility; the earth was coming alive again and the ceremonies were essentially festive occasions from which the Maypole Dances and Garland Days are happy survivals. After the gaiety came the purification or spring cleaning. The preparations were for the most important feast of the pagan year, the Midsummer Festival, and it was in readiness for this that the temples and houses were swept out and the soiled floor rushes replaced with newly grown, sweet-smelling ones.

Over the centuries pagan legends mingled with Christian beliefs and the powers of the hawthorn were reattributed to its use for the Crown of Thorns. The scent of may blossoms, delicious out of doors, can be overpowering and oppressive when brought inside; few people, even if they know of its association with death, realize that the flowers supposedly carry the smell of the great plague of the fourteenth century, as a permanent reminder of the horrors of the Black Death.

The potentially malicious influence of the elder is mentioned in the chapter on berries, but it is reassuring that the spirits only react if their wood is misused. In Scotland, a sprig of elderflower tucked into a horse's bridle ensures a good crop of hay and any countryman who wishes to ward off the evil eye from himself and his farm wears some of the flowers in his cap.

GREEN SPRING SOUP

SERVES SIX TO EIGHT

225 g/8 oz sorrel leaves
125 g/4 oz spring onions or
shallots
125 g/4 oz parsley

225 g/8 oz spinach leaves
1 litre/2 pints bacon or ham
stock
25 g/1 oz flour

Optional
2 eggs

150 ml/¼ pint cream

Wash the sorrel, spinach and parsley, removing any tough ribs and stems. Add with chopped onions or shallots to ½ litre (1 pint) hot stock and simmer for 6 minutes. Liquidize with the flour and return to a clean pan. Add the remaining stock and cook for a further 4–5 minutes. Season.

To serve cold
Chill well and swirl in a spoonful of cream before serving.

To serve hot
Beat 2 egg yolks with 150 ml (¼ pint) cream and gradually add a little hot soup. Mix well. Return to saucepan and reheat stirring. Do not allow to boil.
Serve with plenty of finely milled parsley on top.

SORREL AND RICE SOUP

SERVES SIX TO EIGHT

50 g/2 oz sorrel leaves
50 g/2 oz Patna rice
1 litre/2 pints chicken stock

275 ml/½ pint milk
1 egg
salt, pepper
pinch freshly ground nutmeg

Finely chop sorrel leaves and add them with the rice to the chicken stock. Bring to the boil and simmer for approximately 12 minutes until the rice is cooked. Add milk, seasoning and beaten egg and reheat gently. Do not allow to boil.

NETTLE SOUP

SERVES FOUR

225 g/8 oz young nettle tops　　*½ litre/1 pint milk*
1 tablespoon potato flour　　　*salt, pepper*

Use gloves to pick the nettles which should not be more than 18 cm (6–8 inches) high. Wash the leaves thoroughly, discarding any stems. Put these into a saucepan over low heat and allow them to cook gently into a mush, for about 10 minutes. Add hot milk and potato flour worked into a smooth paste with a little water. Cook, stirring until thickened. Sieve and season to taste.

NETTLE BROTH

SERVES FOUR

225 g/8 oz young nettle tops　　*½ litre/1 pint chicken stock*
50 g/2 oz barley　　　　　　　*salt, pepper*
　　　　　　　　　　　　　　　croutons

Pick the leaves from the stalks and liquidize with 150 ml (¼ pint) of the chicken stock; set aside. Simmer the barley in the remaining stock until tender. Add the nettles and continue cooking for a further 10 minutes. Check seasoning and serve very hot garnished with croutons.

SORREL PURÉE

225 g/8 oz sorrel leaves

Wash the leaves, removing any large ribs. Chop and boil them in a small amount of water for a few minutes. Drain and sieve.

For an omelette filling
Reheat purée with a knob of butter. Season and add to omelette just before serving.

For a sauce

Add 2 tablespoonfuls purée to ½ litre (1 pint) well-seasoned white sauce. Enrich with 2 tablespoonfuls cream.

Serve with veal; the sharp flavour also makes an excellent foil to such fish as mackerel and herring.

SORREL SOUFFLÉ

SERVES THREE

3 tablespoons sorrel purée	*25 g/1 oz butter*
25 g/1 oz flour	*260 ml/bare ½ pint milk*
3 eggs	*50 g/2 oz grated Parmesan*
pepper, salt	*cheese*

Butter an 18-cm (7-inch) soufflé dish. Melt the butter and stir in the flour. Cook for 2–3 minutes and add the sorrel purée. Cook for a further few minutes mixing well. Gradually add milk and stir until thick. Separate the eggs. Remove the sauce from the heat and beat in the egg yolks, one at a time. Add seasoning and all but one tablespoon of cheese. Whip the egg whites and fold thoroughly into the mixture. Pour into a soufflé dish and sprinkle the remaining cheese on top. Bake in a hot oven (380° F, 195° C or Gas no. 5½) for 30 minutes until well risen and golden brown on top.

Serve immediately.

HERB CHEESE

225 g/8 oz cream cheese	*2 tablespoons finely chopped*
1 clove garlic	*chives, thyme and parsley*
sea salt	

Place the cream cheese in a large bowl and beat until creamy, adding a little single cream or top of the milk if necessary. Crush the garlic with a teaspoonful of salt and add with the herbs to the cheese. Mix well together and season with more salt if required.

Try putting a knob of herb cheese into halved baked potatoes 5 minutes before serving.

EASTER HERB PUDDING

SERVES FOUR

4 handfuls of available young herbs: nettle tops, sorrel, dandelion leaves, violet leaves and, if possible, the Easter Dock (Polygonum bistorta), traditionally the main ingredient

4 shallots or spring onions	*1 egg*
1 handful oatmeal	*25 g/1 oz butter*

Remove any coarse ribs or damaged leaves from the herbs. Place the herbs and the finely chopped shallots in a saucepan with a small amount of water. Boil until tender and sprinkle in the oatmeal. Simmer, stirring, for 10 minutes. Season. Mix in the beaten egg and butter and turn into a greased ovenproof dish. Bake until hot through.

There are a number of recipes for this traditional Lenten dish which originates from the Lake District and Yorkshire. It makes use of the early green herbs at a time when fresh vegetables are scarce and expensive, and it is a good family supper dish to accompany bacon and egg or sausages.

MINT AND EGG PIE

SERVES FOUR

175 g/6 oz short crust pastry	*3 tablespoons finely chopped mint*
5–6 eggs	*salt, pepper*

Line a pie plate with half the pastry. Break onto this enough whole eggs to cover. Season well and sprinkle with mint. Cover with the remaining pastry. Brush with beaten egg and bake in a preheated oven (400° F, 200° C or Gas no. 6) for 30 minutes. Serve hot or cold. This pie makes excellent picnic food.

HEDGEROW SALAD

*dandelion and sorrel leaves
    as available*
3 tablespoons olive oil
1 tablespoon lemon juice

*salt, pinch sugar, freshly ground
    black pepper*
1 dandelion flower

Allow approximately 75 g/3 oz young leaves per person. Wash well and place in the ice box or salad drawer of the refrigerator for several hours to crisp.

Make a dressing of the oil, lemon juice and seasonings. Just before required, toss the crisped leaves in the dressing and scatter dandelion petals over the salad.

HERB BREAD

275 ml/½ pint milk
450 g/1 lb strong white flour
1 teaspoon salt
2 tablespoons cooking oil

1 egg
10 g/½ oz dried yeast
1 teaspoon sugar
1 tablespoon dry mustard

*4 tablespoons finely milled fresh herbs: parsley, chives, thyme,
    mint, as available.*

Warm the milk to blood heat. Put the yeast and sugar in a warmed basin and lightly beat in half the milk; set aside until mixture bubbles, approximately 10 minutes, depending on temperature of kitchen.

Sift the flour, salt and mustard into a warmed bowl. Make a well in the centre and add the beaten egg and all the remaining ingredients. Knead thoroughly until the dough is elastic and smooth and leaves the bowl cleanly. Cover and leave to rise.

When the dough has doubled in bulk (after approximately 45 minutes), knead again. Shape into a long Vienna loaf and place on baking sheet. Cover and allow to prove for 20–30 minutes. Brush with beaten egg and bake in preheated hot oven (425° F, 220° C or Gas no. 7) for approximately 40 minutes.

A tap on the base of the loaf will sound hollow when the bread is cooked.

QUICK FRENCH HERB BREAD

1 French loaf
salt
125 g/4 oz butter

1 clove garlic
2 tablespoons finely milled
 mixed herbs as above recipe

Soften the butter. Crush a peeled clove of garlic with the salt and beat into the butter together with the herbs.

Slice the French loaf diagonally into 4 cm (1½ inch) thick slices leaving the base intact. Spread butter on each side of every slice. Brush top with oil and crisp in hot oven (425° F, 220° C or Gas no. 7) for a few minutes before serving.

HERBY PIE

A CORNISH DISH FOR FOUR

2 good bunches of parsley
bunch chives or 6 spring
 onions
1 handful beet leaves
2 eggs

milk
1 handful sorrel (or spinach)
(1 lemon if spinach is used)
2 lettuces
125 g/2 oz flour

Remove the parsley stems and any tough ribs from the leaves. Chop all the green items and throw into boiling water for 3 minutes. Drain. Chop the herbs finely and add the grated lemon rind, salt, pepper and the juice of ½ lemon. Put in a greased shallow oven dish.

Sift the flour with a pinch of salt and beat in the eggs; add sufficient milk to give the batter a consistency of thick cream. Pour over the herbs and bake in a preheated oven (350° F, 180° C or Gas no. 4) for 30 minutes.

Serve with grilled tomatoes and bacon. The pie looks attractive turned out and should be served cut in wedges like a cake.

ELDERFLOWER FRITTERS

125 g/4 oz flour
2 eggs
275 ml/½ pint milk
deep fat for frying

50 g/2 oz castor sugar
1 tablespoon vegetable oil
elderflower heads—allow two
    per person

Sift the flour into a large basin and add sugar. Mix in one egg, the yolk of the second egg and the oil, plus sufficient milk to give the batter the consistency of thick cream. Beat well. Just before using add the stiffly beaten second egg white.

Holding the elderflower heads by the stem, dip them into the batter and plunge at once into the hot fat. Fry for a few minutes until the flowers are coloured; drain well and dust with icing sugar.

Serve hot.

MINT SORBET

SERVES SIX

425 ml/¾ pint water
2 lemons
green colouring
1 handful of fresh mint leaves

125 g/4 oz sugar
1 egg white
3 grapefruit
crystallized mint leaves

Dissolve the sugar in water. Add the rind from both lemons and boil for 5 minutes. Pour this over the chopped mint leaves and leave until cold. Add lemon juice and strain into freezer container. Freeze until the edges are firm. Turn into a large bowl, add beaten egg white and whisk all together until light. Return to lidded container and freeze until firm.

To serve
Cut the grapefruit in half and remove all the flesh and membrane leaving a smooth shell. Cut sections of fruit from the membrane and put a few in the base of each shell; sprinkle with sugar and chill. Place a spoonful of the sorbet in each grapefruit half and decorate with crystallized mint leaves.

MINT ICE CREAM

SERVES FOUR

150 ml/¼ pint water
1 lemon
1 handful of fresh mint leaves
  picked from the stem

125 g/4 oz sugar
150 ml/¼ pint double cream
green colouring

Place the sugar, water and lemon rind in a saucepan. Bring slowly to the boil, stirring until the sugar is dissolved. Simmer for 3 minutes and pour over finely chopped mint leaves. Add the lemon juice. Cool. Strain into an ice tray and place in the freezer compartment until it begins to freeze round the edge. Turn into a large bowl and beat until mushy. Fold in the lightly whipped cream and enough colouring to give a cool, fresh green. Place in a covered container and freeze until firm.

MINT PASTY

For the pastry
  150 g/5 oz hard margarine
  225 g/8 oz plain flour
  1 egg
  2 level tablespoons castor sugar
  water to mix

For the filling
  50 g/2 oz butter
  25 g/1 oz soft brown sugar
  175 g/6 oz raisins
  4 tablespoons chopped mint

Put the margarine in the refrigerator freezer for 10 minutes. Grate margarine coarsely into the sifted flour. Add an egg yolk, 1 tablespoon sugar and water to mix. Knead lightly and leave to cool for 30 minutes.

Cream the butter and sugar until light. Add the raisins and chopped mint and mix all well together. Line a shallow 20 cm (8 inch) pie plate with half the pastry. Fill to within an inch of the edge; cover with remaining pastry. Brush with egg white and sprinkle with castor sugar. Bake in a preheated oven (425° F, 220° C or Gas no. 7) for 10 minutes; reduce temperature to 350° F (180° C or Gas no. 4) and cook for 20–30 minutes. Serve warm.

25

SPRING MINT PRESERVE

FOR USE INSTEAD OF MINT SAUCE

¾ kg/1½ lb gooseberries *450 g/1 lb sugar*
160 ml/⅓ pint cider vinegar *2 large bunches mint*

Top and tail the gooseberries. Cook them gently in vinegar with a bunch of mint until tender; do not overcook. Discard the mint, add the sugar, and stir until dissolved. Cook until thick stirring constantly. Add the chopped mint from the second bunch. Mix well and pot in small jars.

This makes a much more interesting accompaniment to lamb than the conventional liquid mint sauce.

AUTUMN MINT PRESERVE

FOR USE INSTEAD OF MINT SAUCE

1 kg/2 lb apples *350 g/¾ lb sugar to every*
large bunch mint *½ litre/1 pint of purée*

Chop the apples roughly and simmer gently in the minimum water to prevent burning. When soft, sieve and measure the purée. Return to a clean pan and add 350 g (¾ lb) sugar for each ½ litre (1 pint) of apple. Stir over medium heat until dissolved and boil until set.

Stir in finely chopped mint leaves and pot in warmed jars.

MINT VINEGAR

cider vinegar *bunch freshly picked mint*

Pack a widemouthed jar half full with mint leaves. Pour cold vinegar over and store for 6 weeks, shaking the bottle daily. Strain carefully and bottle.

This makes an excellent base for mint sauce or any mint flavoured dressings.

Herb vinegars are considered to have many therapeutic properties and drunk daily are an excellent tonic to the system. Dilute 2 teaspoonfuls in a glass of hot water and drink before breakfast. Sweeten to taste with honey if preferred.

MINT JELLY

1½ kg/3 lb cooking apples   *¾ litre/1½ pints water*
1 lemon   *sugar*
large bunch fresh mint

Roughly chop the apples and put in a preserving pan with the water and pared lemon rind. Simmer until the fruit is soft and turn into a jelly bag to drip overnight.

Measure the juice and for each ½ litre (1 pint) allow ½ kg (1 lb) sugar. Place in pan with strained lemon juice and bring to the boil, stirring until the sugar is dissolved. Add the bunch of mint, stems tied together for easy removal, and boil until setting point is reached. Discard the mint.

Check the colour of the jelly and if necessary add a little green colouring. Finely chopped fresh mint leaves can be added at this stage. Pot and seal.

MINT CHUTNEY

½ kg/1 lb onions   *½ kg/1 lb apples*
½ kg/1 lb raisins   *good handful mint leaves*
2 teaspoons salt   *2 teaspoons mustard*
¾ litre/1½ pints vinegar   *1½ teaspoons sugar*

Using an enamel or aluminium saucepan dissolve the sugar in half the vinegar and add mustard and salt. Peel and core the apples and put them through the mincer with the onions, raisins and mint leaves. Add, together with all the remaining ingredients, to the hot vinegar. Boil gently for 20 minutes stirring occasionally. Pot in warmed jars and seal with synthetic skin.

Leave to mature for 2 months before using.

27

MUSCAT JELLY

1 kg/2 lb gooseberries   *½ litre/1 pint water*
sugar   *4–6 elderflower heads*

Wash the gooseberries and put them in a casserole with water. Cover and place in a slow oven until the fruit is pale and tender, approximately 2 hours. Pour into a jelly bag and leave to drain overnight.

Measure the juice and allow ½ kg (1 lb) sugar to each ½ litre (pint). Bring the juice and sugar slowly to boil, stirring until the sugar is dissolved. Boil until setting point is reached and remove from the heat. Tie the elderflower heads in muslin and stir round in the hot jelly for several minutes. Remove the flowers and pot the jelly in the usual way.

The combination of elderflowers with gooseberries gives a very delicate flavour, suggesting muscat grapes rather than the more commonplace ingredients.

MUSCAT SYRUP

2 kg/4 lbs gooseberries   *½ litre/1 pint water*
1½ kg/3 lb sugar   *6 heads of elderflowers*

Place the gooseberries and water in a large saucepan and simmer until tender, approximately 10 minutes. Add the warmed sugar. Stir till dissolved and bring to the boil. Remove from heat. Tie the elderflower heads in muslin and leave to infuse in the syrup for 20 minutes. Strain through a nylon jelly bag and pour into warm clean bottles.

Sieve the gooseberries and use for a fool or crumble.

This syrup will keep for a month in the refrigerator. However its scented fragrance has so many delicious uses that it is worth making a quantity; in this case the filled bottles should be sterilized for 10 minutes—for the method see recipe for Blackberry Ketchup, page 68.

Ideas for serving

Use the syrup for sprinkling over trifle sponge, for a sorbet or as the basis of a fruit salad.

MINT JULEP

¼ litre/½ pint unsweetened orange juice
large bunch fresh mint
3 bottles dry ginger ale

3 lemons
125 g/¼ lb castor sugar
sprigs of mint for garnish

Bruise the mint leaves and put in a basin with the juice of 2 lemons, the sugar and orange juice. Leave to infuse for 2 hours, then strain.

Put plenty of ice cubes into a bowl and pour over the mint infusion and ginger ale. Garnish with sprigs of mint and sliced lemon. Imbibe with a straw.

Although this drink is associated with the southern United States, versions of it were known in the Middle East four centuries ago. Sophisticated drinkers can base their Julep on whisky, rum or brandy, but returning from a country foray this simple recipe would be welcome and refreshing.

NETTLE BEER

approximately 9 litres/2 gallons young nettle tops (when lightly pressed down)
9 litres/2 gallons water
40 g/1¾ oz cream of tartar

1 kg/2 lbs granulated sugar
25 g/1 oz yeast

Wash the nettles and boil in water for 20 minutes. Put the sugar and cream of tartar into a large earthenware or plastic container. Strain the nettle liquid over them. Stir to dissolve the sugar and allow to cool to approximately 21° C (70° F). Sprinkle the yeast over. Cover and leave for 24 hours.

Siphon carefully into bottles so as not to disturb the sediment. Cork.

It is ready to drink in about 48 hours.

DANDELION WINE

MAKES SIX BOTTLES

2 litres/2 quarts dandelion heads	*4 oranges*
	1½ kg/3 lb sugar
4½ litres/1 gallon water	*1 teaspoon wine yeast*
1 Campden tablet	*1 teaspoon yeast nutrient*

The flowers should be gathered on a sunny day when they are fully out and should be used as soon as possible after picking. Look them over carefully, discarding any green. Place them in a bowl and pour on boiling water. Cover. When cool add 1 Campden tablet and leave for 2 days.

Peel the oranges avoiding the white pith. Bring the peel and dandelion mixture to the boil. Boil for 5 minutes and strain on to the sugar. Stir well, cover and leave to cool. When the temperature is approximately 21°C (70°F) add the strained orange juice, wine yeast and nutrient. Pour into a fermentation jar and top up with boiled water if necessary. Fit the air-lock. Rack and bottle as usual when fermentation has ceased.

This is deservedly one of the great classic country wines but it is not the easiest to make and the recipe should be closely followed.

Keep for 6 months and serve slightly chilled.

SPRING HERB WINE

350 g/12 oz parsley	*125 g/4 oz mint leaves*
1 lemon	*50 g/2 oz thyme*
2 kg/4 lb granulated sugar	*25 g/1 oz piece root ginger (optional)*
4½ litres/gallon water	
1 tablespoon strong tea	*1 teaspoon each of wine yeast and yeast nutrient*

Pick the herbs on a dry day and strip the leaves gently from their stalks to avoid bruising them. Simmer the leaves in 1 litre (1 quart) of water for half an hour.

Place sliced lemon, bruised ginger and sugar in a large container. Pour on boiling herb water and stir until sugar is dissolved. Add remaining water and tea. When cooled to 21° C (70° F) add yeast and yeast nutrient. Stir well and cover closely. Leave for 24 hours. Strain into a fermenting jar and fit the air-lock.

When fermenting has finished, siphon off into a storage jar in the usual way. Leave for 6 months and bottle.

Drink this wine as an aperitif in order to enjoy its special fragrance.

ELDERFLOWER CHAMPAGNE

4 clusters of elderflowers picked on a dry sunny day
2 tablespoons white vinegar   1 lemon
¾ kg/1½ lb granulated sugar   4½ litres/1 gallon cold water

Peel the lemon thinly and squeeze the juice. Put with the other ingredients into a large jug or basin. Stir to dissolve the sugar. Cover with a cloth and leave to stand for 24 hours. Strain and pour into screw top bottles; screw down tightly. Depending on the temperature, it will be ready in 10 to 21 days when the natural yeast will have produced a sparkling drink. Serve chilled.

Generations of country people have made this delicious non-alcoholic drink. Only with the arrival of the Trade Descriptions Act have the cautious referred to it as 'elderade'.

The greedy should be warned that it is mildly diuretic.

HAWTHORN LIQUEUR

brandy   *white hawthorn flowers*
castor sugar

This is a method rather than a recipe. Although the use of brandy sounds extravagant, the addition of sugar makes the brandy go further and the unusual delectable result will disarm critics.

Much of the success depends on careful preparation of the flowers. They should be picked after 12 o'clock on a sunny day when the overnight dew has dried.

Remove the petals, discarding all the rest of the flower. Loosely fill a bottle with the petals and sprinkle in 50 g (2 oz) castor sugar. Fill up with brandy and cork well. Shake occasionally until the sugar has dissolved.

Leave for 3 months. Strain carefully through muslin, twice if necessary.

Retain the petals to scatter in trifles.

Serve the brandy as a liqueur. In hot weather enjoy it diluted with soda water and ice.

PRESERVED PETALS

gum arabic and rosewater   *castor sugar*
  (obtainable from chemist)

Place 1 teaspoonful of gum arabic with 1 tablespoon of rosewater in a small screw top bottle. Leave to dissolve for a few days, shaking the bottle occasionally.

Pick the flowers and leaves on a warm day so that they are as dry as possible. Using a fine brush, paint each flower evenly taking care that both sides and every part is covered by the solution. Place on a wire cake tray and dredge with caster sugar. Put in a warm place such as an airing cupboard or oven plate drawer to complete the drying.

Small flowers such as primroses and violets are the most successful for this treatment. The preserved flowers look delightful used as cake decoration and should be placed in groups on white glacé icing before it sets; a few stalks cut from candied angelica complete the picture.

Preserved mint leaves are very useful to have in the store cupboard. Like the flowers, they retain their flavour when preserved and give a distinct lift when used as a garnish for grapefruit, fruit salads or ices.

If gum arabic is difficult to find, similar results can be obtained using a lightly beaten egg white. The flowers or leaves should be dipped in the solution, dredged with sugar and dried carefully as in the method given above.

Store in the dark in a lidded container where they will keep satisfactorily for several months.

MUSHROOMS

It is only in the last hundred years that botanists have understood the life-cycle of mushrooms, and their curious growth habits have ensured a plentiful supply of legends. The fact that they appear overnight, have no flowers, leaves or seeds and frequently disintegrate into a black liquid mass, adds to their mystical and evil reputation. It is remarkable that in spite of these apparent disadvantages, fungi have been eaten and enjoyed for some three hundred years.

Many of the myths surrounding fungi concern the problems of identifying beyond doubt those that are edible. The most repeated advice that a poisonous species will turn a silver spoon black was first recorded in the 4th century BC; age has not made the story any more reliable. The only safeguard is to learn the characteristics of edible species, ideally from a naturalist but, failing that, from a good field guide.

Although the mushroom is not a conventional hedgerow plant, the following recipes have been made from field mushrooms gathered from a roadside verge, and horse mushrooms well hidden in deep grass between racehorse gallops and a public path. It is unexpected finds such as these that make a country walk exciting.

CREAM OF MUSHROOM SOUP

SERVES FOUR

225 g/½ lb mushrooms (the stems only will do very well for this soup)
1 onion   *850 ml/1½ pints chicken stock*
75 g/3 oz butter   *40 g/1½ oz flour*
150 ml/¼ pint single cream   *pepper, salt and nutmeg*

Chop the onion and mushrooms and sauté in butter. Stir in the flour and cook for a further 3 minutes. Gradually add the hot stock. Simmer for 10 minutes and liquidize or sieve. Season to taste with freshly ground black pepper, salt and a pinch of nutmeg.

Stir in the cream and serve.

CLEAR MUSHROOM SOUP

SERVES FOUR

225 g/½ lb mushrooms   *850 ml/1½ pints good beef stock*
seasoning   *croutons*

Chop the mushroom stems finely and slice the caps. Simmer these in stock for 30 minutes. Check the seasoning and serve garnished with croutons.

This makes a lighter start to a meal than the more conventional cream of mushroom soup.

STUFFED MUSHROOMS (1)

COLD HORS-D'OEUVRE FOR SIX

*12 or 18 open mushrooms
depending on size
225 g/½ lb cottage cheese
1 teaspoon curry powder*

*2 tablespoon chives
salt, freshly ground black
pepper
paprika and lettuce,
for garnish*

Wipe the mushrooms carefully with a damp cloth and remove the stems. Blend together the cheese, finely chopped chives and seasonings. Fill the caps with the mixture and dust with paprika. Serve on lettuce.

STUFFED MUSHROOMS (2)

HOT HORS-D'OEUVRE FOR SIX

*12 large mushrooms
3 shallots
50 g/2 oz butter
50 g/2 oz chopped ham
cooking oil
150 g/5 oz fresh breadcrumbs*

*1 tablespoon finely milled parsley
1 clove garlic
1 dessertspoon tomato purée
diluted with 2–3 tablespoons
water
12 rounds fried bread*

Clean the mushrooms and remove the stems. Arrange the caps in a large greased baking dish. Mince the shallots and sauté with the crushed clove of garlic in butter until transparent. Add the finely chopped mushroom stems and cook for a further few minutes. Reserve 25 g (1 oz) of breadcrumbs and stir all the remaining ingredients into the mushroom mixture. Season well. Fill the caps and cover with the remaining breadcrumbs fried in butter. Bake in a hot oven (400° F, 200° C or Gas no. 6) for 15 minutes.
Serve on rounds of fried bread.

DEVILLED MUSHROOMS

SERVES FOUR

450 g/1 lb mushrooms
4 slices toast

50 g/2 oz butter
seasoning, lemon juice

For the sauce
150 ml/¼ pint double cream
1 tablespoon tomato ketchup
1 tablespoon Worcester sauce

1 tablespoon Harvey's Sauce
salt, pepper, freshly grated nutmeg
dash of cayenne

Wipe the mushrooms and cut the stems level with the cups. Heat the butter in a frying pan and fry the mushrooms quickly, a few at a time. Lay them in a greased casserole and season with salt, pepper and lemon juice.

Whip the cream until stiff. Add in all ingredients by degrees, whisking gently to keep sauce as thick as possible. Spread the sauce over the mushrooms and bake in a pre-heated hot oven (400° F, 200° C or Gas no. 6) for 10 minutes until brown and bubbling.

Serve immediately garnished with triangles of toast.

MUSHROOMS À LA TUNISIENNE

COLD HORS-D'OEUVRE FOR FOUR

225 g/½ lb small mushrooms
1½ tablespoons concentrated
  tomato purée
bouquet garni of bay leaf,
  thyme and parsley

2 tablespoons olive oil
juice of ½ lemon
salt, freshly ground pepper
lettuce leaves and paprika
  for garnish

Place all the ingredients except the mushrooms in a shallow pan. Mix them well and bring gently to the boil. Simmer for 3 minutes. Add the sliced mushrooms. Cover and cook over a low heat for 10 minutes, shaking the pan from time to time. Remove the bouquet garni and let the mushrooms cool in the sauce.

Serve on lettuce leaves and dust with paprika.

MUSHROOMS À LA GRECQUE

COLD HORS-D'OEUVRE FOR FOUR

2 shallots
225 g/½ lb button mushrooms
juice of 1 lemon
150 ml/¼ pint white wine
2 tablespoons olive oil

1 clove garlic
bouquet garni of bay leaf, thyme
and parsley
2 tablespoons finely milled
parsley for garnish

Chop the shallots and crush the clove of garlic. Place all the ingredients except the mushrooms in a saucepan and simmer for 5 minutes. Quarter the mushrooms and add to the pan. Simmer for a further 5 minutes. Remove the mushrooms to a serving dish and boil the liquid to reduce by half. Take out the bouquet garni and pour the liquid over the mushrooms.

Serve cold, garnished with plenty of parsley.

MUSHROOM SALAD

SERVES TWO

125 g/4 oz mushrooms
chives

lettuce

For the French dressing
3 tablespoons oil
1 tablespoon lemon juice

salt, pepper

Wipe over the mushrooms. Cut off the stalks and slice the mushrooms into a bowl. Mix together the oil, lemon juice and seasoning and toss the mushrooms lightly in the mixture. Chill. Line a salad bowl with lettuce and add the drained mushrooms. Sprinkle liberally with finely chopped chives and, if available, add several of the flower heads for colour.

Sliced raw mushrooms are a most distinctive addition to all mixed salads. There is no need to peel them but they must be well examined for insect life; for this reason it is often necessary to discard the stalks of wild fungi.

MUSHROOM AND BEAN SALAD

SERVES SIX TO EIGHT

225 g/8 oz kidney beans	*oil*
225 g/8 oz mushrooms	*2 onions*
2 tablespoons milled	*2 cloves garlic*
parsley	*French dressing*

Soak the beans in cold water overnight or, alternatively, cover the beans with boiling water and leave for 2 hours.

Peel and chop the onions and sauté in a little oil until transparent. Drain the beans and add to the pan. Cover them with boiling water and simmer until tender, approximately 2¼ hours. (Use a pressure cooker if available which will reduce the time to 15–20 minutes.) Drain well.

Chop the mushrooms and add them with the parsley to the beans. Pour over a well-seasoned French dressing and mix all together thoroughly. Chill.

To serve, arrange the beans and mushrooms in a lettuce lined salad bowl and garnish with very thin, raw onion rings.

The addition of mushrooms gives a lighter texture to an otherwise rather substantial salad. It can either be used as a starter to the meal or to accompany cold meat.

MUSHROOM PÂTÉ

SERVES FOUR

3 shallots	*50 g/2 oz butter*
½ teaspoon ground allspice	*150 ml/¼ pint milk*
225 g/½ lb mushrooms	*1 clove garlic*
2 thick slices crustless brown	*seasoning*
bread	*lemon juice*

Chop the shallots finely and sauté gently in butter until they are transparent. Crush a clove of garlic with a little salt and add to the pan together with the allspice and roughly chopped mushrooms. Cook, stirring gently for 4–5 minutes.

Soak the bread in the milk for a few minutes; squeeze out and crumble into the mushroom mixture. Fry together for a further 2–3 minutes and remove from the heat. Season carefully with freshly ground black pepper, a squeeze of lemon juice and plenty of salt. Pass the mixture through a mouli or medium mincer and pack into a terrine. Chill for 24 hours.

Serve as a starter with toast, or as a light supper dish with hot herb bread (see recipes pages 22, 23).

MUSHROOM SOUFFLÉ

SERVES THREE

225 g/8 oz mushrooms	*275 ml/½ pint chicken stock*
75 g/3 oz butter	*3 egg yolks, large*
50 g/2 oz flour	*3 egg whites, large*
2 shallots	

Grease thoroughly a litre (2 pint) soufflé dish. Slice thinly 50 g (2 oz) of mushroom caps; chop the remainder finely. Sauté the chopped shallots in 25 g (1 oz) of butter until transparent. Add the chopped mushrooms and cook for 3–4 minutes while stirring.

Put the remaining butter, flour and stock into a saucepan. With a balloon whisk, beat continually over a moderate heat until boiling; cook for 3 minutes and set aside to cool slightly. Whisk in the egg yolks one at a time and stir in thoroughly the chopped mushroom mixture. Season well.

Beat the egg whites until stiff and cut and fold carefully into the sauce. Pour half the mixture into the soufflé dish; scatter over the reserved sliced mushrooms, and pour the rest of the soufflé mixture over them.

Bake in a pre-heated oven (375° F, 190° C or Gas no. 5) for approximately 40 minutes until well risen and brown.

Serve immediately.

MUSHROOM AND EGG BAKE

SERVES FOUR

1 onion
125 g/4 oz mushrooms
50 g/2 oz butter
1½ tablespoons mushroom
  ketchup (see recipe page 48)

6 hardboiled eggs
275 ml/½ pint bechamel sauce
paprika, parsley, pepper and
  salt

Sauté the finely chopped onion in butter until it is transparent. Add the roughly chopped mushrooms and fry for a few more minutes. Put in a greased shallow ovenproof dish and arrange halved hardboiled eggs on top. Add the mushroom ketchup to the bechamel sauce and pour this over the egg and mushroom base. Sprinkle the top with paprika and bake in a moderate oven to heat through thoroughly.

With an edging of mashed potato this makes a substantial supper dish.

SAVOURY MUSHROOM PIE

SERVES FOUR

175 g/6 oz short crust pastry
2 onions
50 g/2 oz flour
450 g/1 lb hard cabbage

275 ml/½ pint stock
225 g/½ lb mushrooms
125 g/4 oz butter
1 tablespoon chopped fresh
  parsley and chives

Peel and chop the onions and sauté them in 25 g (1 oz) butter in a large saucepan. Add the shredded cabbage and cook together for several minutes. Mix in the sliced mushrooms, adding a further knob of butter if necessary. Stew for 3–4 minutes. Drain the vegetables adding the liquid to the heated stock.

Make a thick sauce with 25 g (1 oz) butter, 25 g (1 oz) flour and the stock. Season the vegetables, mix in the herbs and add them to the sauce. Stir well together and transfer to a greased vegetable pie dish. Cover the dish with pastry and bake in a hot oven (400° F, 200° C or Gas no. 6) for 40 minutes.

MUSHROOM AND PRAWN FLAN

SERVES FOUR

20 cm/8 inch flan case	*275 ml/½ pint milk*
125 g/4 oz prawns	*salt, pepper*
2 eggs	*parsley*
25 g/1 oz butter	*lemon for garnish*
125 g/4 oz mushrooms	

Sauté the chopped mushrooms in butter for 3–4 minutes. Add the prawns and spread evenly over the base of a pastry case. Lightly beat the eggs and add milk and seasoning. Pour carefully into the flan. Bake in a preheated oven (375° F, 190° C or Gas no. 5) for about 30 minutes or until the filling is set.

Serve hot, garnished with parsley and lemon, or cold with salad.

MUSHROOM SMETANA

SERVES FOUR

1 onion	*150 ml/¼ pint sour cream*
1 clove garlic	*1 tablespoon brandy*
50 g/2 oz butter	*seasoning*
225 g/½ lb mushrooms	*parsley to garnish*

Melt the butter in a large pan and cook the finely chopped onion and crushed garlic until transparent. Slice the mushrooms thinly and add to the pan. Cover and cook for approximately 5 minutes until the mushrooms are tender. Stir in the cream and brandy. Season. Cook for a further few minutes until very hot.

Served with boiled rice, this makes a delicious supper dish. It is also an excellent sauce to accompany veal and fish dishes.

PORK FILLET WITH MUSHROOMS

SERVES EIGHT

1 kg/2 lb pork fillet	*50 g/2 oz butter*
2 onions, medium sized	*225 g/8 oz button mushrooms*
1 dessertspoon paprika	*1 glass sherry*
1 dessertspoon flour	*275 ml/½ pint jellied stock*
1 dessertspoon potato flour	*1 teaspoon tomato purée*
	150 ml/¼ pint sour cream

Cut the fillets into 5 cm (2 inch) pieces. Sauté in butter until coloured and set aside. Fry the finely chopped onions with the paprika for 2 minutes on a low heat. Gradually stir in the flour, tomato purée, sherry and stock and bring to the boil. Replace the pork, cover and simmer gently until tender, for approximately 40 minutes.

Add the mushrooms and the potato flour dissolved in 2 tablespoons cold water. Season to taste. Heat through and swirl sour cream over the surface just before serving.

PLAICE AND MUSHROOM CASSEROLE

SERVES FOUR

8 fillets plaice	*1 lemon and 1 lemon for*
125 g/4 oz mushrooms	*garnish*
4–5 shallots	*½ litre/1 pint parsley sauce*
50 g/2 oz butter	

Sauté the chopped shallots in butter until they are transparent. Add the chopped mushrooms and fry for a further 2–3 minutes. Skin the fillets and sprinkle with pepper, salt and lemon juice. Roll them up and place in a greased casserole. Add the mushroom mixture to the fish, pushing it down between the fillets. Pour over the parsley sauce and bake in a moderate oven (350° F, 180° C or Gas no. 4) for 35 minutes.

Garnish with lemon.

For the parsley sauce
½ litre/1 pint milk
50 g/2 oz butter
salt and pepper

2 tablespoons parsley
50 g/2 oz flour

The sauce can be made very quickly by putting all the ingredients in a blender and switching this on for 1 minute. Then pour the mixture into a saucepan and bring to the boil while stirring. Cook for 2 minutes before pouring over the fish.

PARTRIDGES AND MUSHROOMS

SERVES EIGHT

4 partridges
50 g/2 oz flour
50 g/2 oz butter
1 glass sherry

450 g/1 lb mushrooms
6 shallots
½ litre/pint stock
1 tablespoon rowan jelly (see recipe page 65)

Slice three quarters of the mushrooms. Chop the shallots finely and sauté in butter until they are transparent. Add mushrooms and cook slowly for a further few minutes. Season well and stuff the partridges with the mixture. Put in an open casserole and roast at 375° F (190° C, Gas no. 5) until the birds are browned, approximately 7 minutes. Meanwhile, make the sauce (see below). Add the sauce to the browned partridges and turn the oven down to 300° F (150° C or Gas no. 2), and simmer for ¾ hour until cooked. The exact time will depend on the age of the birds. Add the remaining 125 g (¼ lb) of chopped mushrooms 15 minutes before the end of the cooking.

For the sauce
Melt the butter in a saucepan. Add the flour and cook for 3 minutes stirring well. Gradually add the hot stock and bring to the boil, stirring. Mix in the rowan jelly and sherry and taste for seasoning.

MUSHROOM STUFFING

1 rasher bacon	*2 shallots*
25 g/1 oz butter	*175 g/6 oz fresh breadcrumbs*
175 g/6 oz mushrooms	*75 g/3 oz fresh parsley*
(stems only can be used)	*1 egg*

Dice the bacon and fry in butter with the finely chopped shallots. When cooked, add either minced or chopped mushrooms and fry quickly over a brisk heat for a few minutes. Put the bread and parsley in a blender and reduce to fine crumbs. Add to the mushroom mixture, bind with a beaten egg and season well.

Bake in a greased oven dish to accompany roast pork, or use to stuff chicken or game birds.

SAVOURY PANCAKES

MAKES TWELVE

For the pancakes
125 g/4 oz flour
1 egg plus 1 egg yolk
2 tablespoons cooking oil
275 ml/approx. ½ pint milk
pinch salt

For the filling
50 g/2 oz flour
75 g/3 oz butter
275 ml/½ pint milk
50 g/2 oz mushrooms
125 g/4 oz prawns
1 tablespoon sherry

To finish
single cream
buttered crumbs

1 lemon

To make the pancakes, sift the flour and salt into a bowl. Add the egg, egg yolk, oil and half the milk; beat well until smooth. Gradually add further milk and beat until the batter is the consistency of single cream. Make the pancakes in the usual way, giving the batter a thorough whisk before pouring into the frying pan.

Make a thick binding sauce with 50 g (2 oz) butter, flour and milk. Sauté the chopped mushrooms in the remaining butter for 5 minutes. Mix into the sauce together with the prawns and sherry. Simmer for 10 minutes and season to taste. Spread the mixture onto the pancakes. Roll each one up and place in a shallow greased oven dish. Pour a little single cream over and sprinkle with buttered crumbs. Bake till brown, approximately 25 minutes at 350° F (180° C or Gas no. 4).

Allow two pancakes per person and decorate with lemon quarters and a few extra prawns.

This sauce also makes a delicious filling for vol-au-vent cases.

MUSHROOM RISOTTO

SERVES SIX

350 g/12 oz rice	*50 g/2 oz butter*
1 onion	*575 ml/1 pint hot chicken stock*
50 g/2 oz grated cheese	*125 g/4 oz mushrooms*
1 clove garlic	*bouquet garni*

Optional
125 g/4 oz peas   *½ red pepper*

Melt the butter in a large saucepan and sauté the finely chopped onion and crushed clove of garlic until golden. Add the rice and stir until it is well coated with the butter. Stir in the chopped mushrooms and cook for a further 2–3 minutes before adding the hot stock and bouquet garni. (The peas and diced red pepper can be added now to give colour.) Bring to the boil, stirring. Cover the saucepan and simmer over a very low heat until the rice is cooked and the risotto takes on a creamy texture. Allow 25–30 minutes but keep a close watch on the pan towards the end to prevent the rice catching. Remove the bouquet garni.

Serve immediately with grated cheese.

MUSHROOM KETCHUP

1½ kg/3 lb mushrooms (the giant horse mushrooms are excellent
  for this recipe)
125 g/4 oz salt
1 tablespoon pickling spice
275 ml/½ pint vinegar

275 ml/½ pint red wine
  (optional)
1 small onion

Wipe the mushrooms. Break up into pieces and layer in a crock
with salt. Leave for 3 days in a cool place, stirring the mixture each
day.

Boil the vinegar with the pickling spice and chopped onion for
15 minutes; leave for 24 hours and strain.

On the fourth day add the spiced vinegar to the mushrooms.
Wine can be added at this stage and it greatly enriches the ketchup
if it is used. **Simmer until well reduced, approximately 2½ hours.**
Strain into warm bottles and sterilize for 15 minutes. (For method,
see Blackberry Ketchup page 68.)

Leave for 2–3 months to mature.

Ketchups, or catsups, developed in the late eighteenth and
nineteenth centuries to enliven the numerous meals required
during the long voyages to and from India. Based on vinegar, these
sauces had, and of course still have, the great merit of indefinite
store life. Like chutney, the recipes are flexible and it is fun to
experiment with ingredients until your own family variant
emerges.

PICKLED MUSHROOMS

3 blades bruised mace
25 g/1 oz salt
450 g/1 lb small mushrooms

1 litre/2 pints white malt vinegar
10 g/½ oz black peppercorns,
  roughly crushed

Put the mace, peppercorns, salt and vinegar into an enamel or
aluminium saucepan and bring to the boil. Simmer for 10 minutes
and set aside for 2 hours to infuse. Strain.

Wipe over the mushrooms and trim the stalks level with the caps. Tip the caps into a pan of boiling salted water and boil for 3 minutes. Drain and pack the mushrooms carefully into clean warm jars. Reheat the vinegar and pour boiling over the mushrooms. Tie down with synthetic skin while still hot. Leave to mature for 2–3 months.

DRIED MUSHROOMS

Very occasionally weather conditions combine to produce an outstanding mushroom year; the last one was in 1977 when it was possible to return to the same spot every 24 hours and find it replenished with shining white caps. On these rare occasions it is useful to preserve the fungi in several different ways to vary their ultimate use and keeping time. Mushrooms will be satisfactory from the deep freeze for up to 3 months but if dried will keep for much longer. They are welcome in winter as an enriching addition to stews, sauces and soups.

Method

Wipe the mushrooms carefully and remove their stalks. Thread the caps onto a piece of string alternately with a stiff piece of paper to ensure they do not touch. Hang the strings in a warm place until the mushrooms are shrivelled and completely dry. Suitable gentle heat can be found in the airing cupboard, over a radiator or above the Aga.

Alternatively, place the selected mushrooms in a single layer on wire cake racks and place in a hot plate drawer, an airing cupboard, or use the residual heat from the oven after cooking.

When drying is finished, store in an airtight jar until required.

Revive by soaking the mushrooms overnight in a little water.

Elderberry & Apple Jam

BERRIES RED
AND
BERRIES BLACK

A suitably ancient path in September and October will be edged by hedges throbbing with colour and laden with fruit. The blacks and reds mingle as they share their inherited responsibility, handed down over the centuries, of assisting in the rituals demanded by white and black magic.

Most conspicuous is the elder, a tree whose influence has been so strong that pagan and Christian beliefs concerning it are inextricably mixed. Perhaps it was an elder from which Judas hanged himself; and the strength of the tradition that Christ died on a cross made from elder wood could account for the countryman's persisting reluctance to use it. Even in a hard winter it is an unpopular wood to bring into the house for burning, although the more cynical would maintain that this is because it spits and sparks.

The elder has always been the residence of spirits and their strong territorial feelings transfer to any object made from it. It is therefore most unwise to make a cradle of the wood and thus put a child at the mercy of the Elder Tree Mother, who is reputed to pinch her victims black and blue. But even the most malevolent spirits can be placated by tact: if permission is requested before handling their property no harm will follow. This simple rule allows safe gathering of the enormous crop of berries reliably produced each year. Nicknamed England's grapes, the elderberries give clear indication when they are ready to be picked. As the fruit swells and ripens, the wine-red stalks turn until the berries hang suspended: black, heavy and inviting.

In contrast to the rich black of the elderberries, the bilberry takes on the waxy blue-black colour of the sloe. Bilberry, blaeberry, blueberry or whortleberry are all names for this low-growing, wiry shrub which usually associates with heather on moorland. Like the wild strawberry it is hard to gather more than a handful of berries and the recipes have been chosen to make a small quantity go a long way.

Some of the main constituents of the average hedge are the long trails of briar rose (dog rose) and bramble. The Latin name for the wild rose, *Rosa canina*, dates back to Pliny, the prolific and much quoted writer killed by the eruption of Vesuvius in AD 79. He reported that a soldier bitten by a rabid dog had cured himself by eating the root of this rose. More convincing perhaps to the torn and bleeding gatherer of the colourful hips is the explanation that 'dog' is a corruption of 'dag' or dagger and refers to the formidable thorns.

The blackberry probably produces the most familiar of our wild fruits; all families should indulge in a picking and picnicking expedition when the berries are ripe. Native to this country, it can be found rambling through hedgerows, on commons and in vast clumps from the downs on the south coast of England to the Highlands of Scotland. Its gaelic name 'an druise beannaichte', the blessed bramble, refers to the switch of bramble with which Christ urged on his donkey as He rode to Jerusalem. Botanists are still disputing the exact number of sub-species but there are enough to provide a succession of fruit from August onwards. However, as every countryman knows, the devil spits on the bushes on the 29th September (Michaelmas) and after that the berries are not worth gathering. The satanic anger was roused and thus expressed when the Devil lost his fight with St Michael and was hurled ignominiously out of Heaven.

Apart from the decorative and edible merits of the briar and the bramble, they also provide an unexpected veterinary and medical use and have been associated with cures dating back to pagan times. The long shoots, which root when their tips touch the soil, form a natural and magically powerful arch. It was widely believed, and practised until this century, that certain ailments could be transferred to the living plant if the sufferer, human or animal, crawled backwards and forwards through this loop.

The long, thorny stems have had their strength put to many practical uses too. They were one of the traditional choices for binding the ash sticks which made up the Ashen Faggot—a West Country version of the Yule Log—brought into the house on Christmas Eve. Both their strength and thorns commended them for twining round tombs in the churchyard to discourage restless spirits from emerging. Their use today appears to be confined to those rare bee masters who still practice the art of making a straw skep and use the stripped stem to bind the rolls of straw.

As in all the best stories good will vanquish evil, so in folklore the beneficial influence of a single rowan can outdo all the possible evil emanating from the more prolific elder trees. A rowan or mountain ash in a graveyard prevents the dead from stirring and when placed near a house will provide an all-powerful and year-long protection against fire and evil spirits. Not only is the rowan the sacred tree of the fire god, Thor, but like the may and elder its white blossoms are associated with the mother goddess celebrating the end of winter. In autumn when the heavy crop of berries ripens, they turn scarlet, a colour which is known to be dreaded by witches. Naturally the virtues of such sacred trees are transmitted to the wood. A sprig or cross of rowan twigs is useful to protect both livestock and humans and if it can be incorporated into the making of a cradle or farm wagon there will be long lasting benefit to the owners.

BILBERRY SOUP

SERVES FOUR

450 g/1 lb ripe bilberries
½ litre/1 pint water
sour cream

25 g/1 oz potato flour
sugar to taste

Place the fruit and water in a saucepan and simmer gently for 15 minutes. Sieve and return to a clean pan. Dissolve the potato flour in 2 tablespoons cold water and stir into the fruit to thicken. Sweeten to taste, but be careful to retain the refreshing, slightly tart flavour of the bilberries. Reheat gently.

Serve hot, with a swirl of sour cream in each bowl. In hot weather serve it lightly chilled.

This is a very popular soup in Central Europe where bilberries grow in profusion and from where we import them dried.

CANADIAN BLUEBERRY PIE

SERVES SIX

225 g/8 oz shortcrust pastry
175 g/6 oz soft brown sugar
1 tablespoon lemon juice
450 g/1 lb bilberries

2 tablespoons flour
25 g/1 oz butter
¼ teaspoon cinnamon
pinch salt

Line a 22-cm (9-inch) pie plate with two thirds of the pastry. Mix the flour, cinnamon and sugar together, and sprinkle some of this on the pastry base. Add a layer of berries followed by the sugar mixture, finishing with a top layer of berries. Sprinkle lemon juice over and dot with butter. Cover with a lattice of pastry and bake in a preheated oven (425° F 220° C or Gas no. 7) for 40 minutes.

Serve with vanilla ice cream.

Anyone who has watched their family enjoy this pie will understand why in Yorkshire it is known as Mucky Mouth Pie.

BLACKBERRY FOOL

SERVES FOUR TO SIX

450 g/1 lb blackberries　　　　*125 g/4 oz sugar*
150 ml/¼ pint water　　　　　*15 g/4 oz gelatine*
1 lemon　　　　　　　　　　*150 ml/¼ pint double cream*

Place the fruit, sugar and water in a saucepan over a low heat. Simmer for about 10 minutes until the fruit is tender. Sprinkle the gelatine into 3 tablespoons cold water and leave to soak for a few minutes. Stir the gelatine into the hot fruit until dissolved. Add lemon juice and press the mixture through a nylon sieve. Leave till cold.

Whip the cream until thick and stir into the fruit purée; do not mix in too thoroughly as the whorls of colour add to the attractive appearance of this dish. Chill before serving.

Blackberry purée

In a good blackberry year, a valuable addition to the freezer is sieved blackberry purée (made from the proportions of blackberries, sugar and water given above) in 150 g (¼ pint) quantities. It takes up little space and has many uses. This amount added to an apple pie or apple mousse during the winter gives an excellent flavour of fresh blackberry and apple, or it can be the base for many of the recipes given here.

BLACKBERRY FLUFF

SERVES SIX

ingredients as for Blackberry Fool (above) plus 2 egg whites

For a very light confection for a dinner party try this variation on the fool.

Follow the above recipe for making the purée. Whisk the egg whites until stiff and fold into the cold purée. Stir in whipped cream and pour into glasses. Serve well chilled.

BRAMBLE BAKE

SERVES FOUR

450 g/1 lb ripe blackberries *125 g/4 oz fresh breadcrumbs*
150 ml/¼ pint water *125 g/4 oz sugar*
2 eggs *50 g/2 oz butter*

Grease a 1-litre (2-pint) ovenproof dish. Simmer the blackberries with water for about 10 minutes until tender. Sieve to remove the pips. Stir the sugar and butter into the hot purée until melted. **Mix in the breadcrumbs and the eggs well beaten and pour into the oven dish. Bake at 350° F (180° C or Gas no. 4) for 30 minutes.** Serve hot with cream.

BLACKBERRY AND CHEESE FLAN

SERVES SIX

For the flan case
225 g/8 oz gingernuts *50 g/2 oz castor sugar*
75 g/3 oz unsalted butter

Crush the gingernuts to fine crumbs. This is quickly done in the blender, or place the biscuits between paper and use a rolling pin. Melt the butter and stir in the crumbs and sugar. Mix well and press firmly round a 22-cm (9-inch) flan tin. Put in the refrigerator to harden.

For the filling
225 g/8 oz blackberries, *75 g/3 sugar*
*   plus a few for decoration* *225 g/8 oz cream cheese*
150 ml/¼ pint milk

Sieve the blackberries to remove the pips. Blend with all the other ingredients in a liquidizer and put in the prepared flan case. Decorate with whole berries and chill in the refrigerator until ready to serve.
Note: If using frozen berries you will not need as much milk.

56

BLACKBERRY SORBET

SERVES EIGHT TO TEN

1.4 kg/3 lb blackberries
450 g/1 lb sugar
3 tablespoons Kirsch
   (optional)

850 ml/1½ pints water
2 lemons

Place the berries in a large pan over very low heat until the juice runs. Stir occasionally and simmer until tender. Press through a fine sieve. Cool. Dissolve the sugar in water and bring to the boil. Boil for 2 minutes and leave to cool. When cold, add the purée, strained lemon juice and Kirsch to the syrup. Blend thoroughly and pour into a lidded container.

Freeze until required.

BRAMBLE HAT

SERVES SIX

For the pastry
   225 g/8 oz self-raising flour
   ¼ teaspoon salt
   100 g/3–4 oz shredded suet
   cold water to mix

For the filling
   450 g/1 lb cooking apples
   225 g/8 oz blackberries
   75 g/3 oz demerara sugar

Sieve the flour and salt together and lightly rub in the suet. Add sufficient water to mix to a soft dough. Turn onto a floured board and roll out to a circle 1-cm (¼-inch) thick. Cut out a quarter and line a greased 1-litre (2-pint) pudding basin with the remainder.

Peel, core and slice the apples. Place in the basin alternately with blackberries and sugar. Roll the remaining pastry into a circle and cover the fruit to form a lid. Cover the basin with buttered paper and foil. Steam over constantly simmering water for 3 hours. Unmould carefully.

Serve with custard.

RASPBERRY BRÛLÉE

SERVES FOUR

¾ kg/8 oz raspberries　　　　*275 ml/½ pint double cream*
175 g/6 oz soft brown sugar

Lay the raspberries in a shallow heatproof dish. Whip the cream
until it holds soft peaks and cover the fruit with it. On top of the
cream place 2-cm (½-inch) layer of soft brown sugar. Put this in
the refrigerator for at least 4 hours. When required, place the dish
under a preheated hot grill for 3 minutes and serve at once.

This is undeniably extravagant—and irresistible.

SUMMER PUDDING (1)

SERVES SIX TO EIGHT

Make the day before required.

*¾ kg/1½ lb raspberries, or a mixture of raspberries and
　redcurrants*
175 g/6 oz sugar　　　　*10–12 slices thick white*
175 ml/¼ pint water　　　　*bread*

If using redcurrants, strip the fruit from the stems with a table fork.

Put all the fruit and water into a saucepan. Cover and simmer
gently for 5–7 minutes until the fruit is tender. Add the sugar and
stir until it is dissolved. Set aside to cool.

Trim the crusts from the bread. Line the inside of a 1-litre
(2-pint) pudding basin with neat fingers of bread stood upright.
Spoon in half the fruit, cover with bread, and pour in the
remainder of the fruit and juice. Cover this with the remaining

bread. Put a saucer on top of the pudding, just inside the basin. Press it down gently and put a weight on it. Leave overnight in the refrigerator.

Turn the pudding out onto a serving plate when required and offer cream and sugar to accompany it.

If Madeira cake is used instead of bread it raises the pudding to dinner party status.

This immensely popular pudding was known throughout the nineteenth century as Homeopathic Pudding because doctors considered it a suitably light diet for patients unable to eat pastry.

ROEDGROED MED FLOEDE

SERVES SIX

225 g/8 oz raspberries
225 g/8 oz redcurrants
425 ml/¾ pint water

225 g/8 oz castor sugar
3 rounded tablespoons cornflour
blanched almonds
cream

Place the fruit and water in a saucepan; bring to the boil and simmer covered, until all the juice is extracted, about 10 minutes. Rub through a fine nylon sieve. Return the purée to the saucepan and add the sugar. Mix the cornflour to a paste with cold water and stir this into the hot purée. Cook stirring for 3–4 minutes until thick.

Pour into a glass serving dish. Decorate with split blanched almonds and serve very cold with cream.

This was Queen Alexandra's favourite pudding and it could be called the national pudding of Denmark. Its name sounds more appealing in its original language than the prosaic translation, 'Red Pudding with Cream'. As well as being delicious to eat, it is hard not to indulge in the childish pleasure of attempting the correct pronunciation of its name.

WILD STRAWBERRIES

The tiny wood strawberries are perhaps the most delectable of all fruits, and a mere handful will transform a fresh fruit salad. They are hard to find and when located are unlikely to be gathered in any quantity. They should be treated with the reverence their rarity and delicacy demands. Compliment them with your best glass and silver.

WILD STRAWBERRY SORBET

575 g/1¼ lbs strawberries   *2 egg whites*
275 ml/½ pint water   *175 g/6 oz sugar*
1 lemon

Thinly peel the lemon and put the rind and the sugar with water in a saucepan. Heat slowly until the sugar has dissolved; boil for 5 minutes. Strain and set aside to cool.

Hull the strawberries, reserving a few berries for decoration. Press the remainder through a nylon sieve and add the juice from half the lemon. Whisk the egg whites until very stiff. Combine all the ingredients and mix well.

Put in a lidded container in the freezer. Remove when half frozen, beat well and return to the freezer. Place in the refrigerator 2 hours before required.

Serve in stemmed wine glasses topped with a few whole berries.

STRAWBERRY CHAMPAGNE

Chill the required number of stemmed wine glasses. Divide the hulled strawberries between them. Sprinkle with sieved icing sugar and cover with champagne. Turn the fruit very gently once or twice and chill for 30 minutes.

BILBERRY MUFFINS

MAKES TWELVE MUFFINS

225 g/8 oz self-raising flour *½ teaspoon salt*
1 teaspoon baking powder *2 tablespoons castor sugar*
150 ml/¼ pint approx. milk *1 egg*
2 tablespoons vegetable oil *225 g/8 oz bilberries*

Grease 12 deep patty tins. Sift the flour, salt and baking powder together into a mixing bowl. Stir in the sugar. Beat the egg and add the milk and oil. Add all at once to the dry mixture and stir lightly together. Toss the berries in 1 tablespoon flour and stir quickly into the mixture. Half fill the patty tins and bake in a preheated oven (425° F, 220° C or Gas no. 7) for 25 minutes until well risen and golden brown.

Serve hot with butter.

BILBERRY PRESERVE

450 g/1 lb bilberries *450 g/1 lb sugar*

Place the fruit in a shallow pan and cover with sugar. Leave for several hours to draw the juices. Put into a preserving pan and stir over a low heat until the sugar is dissolved. Boil until just set. Pour into warm jars and cover as usual.

Until comparatively recently the housewife only had her cooking skills to ensure a well-filled larder of fruits and vegetables for the winter months. Preserves presented the fruit more or less whole in a heavy syrup. In Victorian England they were eaten with a teaspoon as they still are on the Continent.

Preserves are an excellent solution for any well-flavoured fruit which is expensive or in short supply.

ROSE DELIGHT

450 g/1 lb apple purée
2 egg whites
cochineal

2 tablespoons rose hip syrup
(see recipe page 63)
2½ tablespoons castor sugar

Towards the end of winter when everyone is tired of the usual apple recipes, tempt jaded palates with this light confection.

Add 2 tablespoons of rose hip syrup to the sweetened apple purée and put in a shallow, ovenproof dish. Whip 2 egg whites until stiff. Fold in 2 tablespoons castor sugar and two drops cochineal to colour them palest pink. Place the mixture over the apple and sprinkle with the remaining sugar. Place in a moderate oven for 20 minutes until the meringue topping is crisp.

BALMORAL SAUCE

rose hips
lemon juice

sugar
rosewater
(obtainable from chemist)

Select large ripe hips, gathered after they have been softened by the first frost.

Remove the tops and cut each hip open to take out all the tiny hairy seeds. Simmer the hips in rosewater till tender. Sieve. Sweeten to taste and add a little lemon juice.

This is reputed to be one of Queen Victoria's favourite sauces and was always served at Balmoral Castle in the autumn. The authentic recipe is very fiddly and time-consuming to prepare. Very similar and much quicker results can be obtained by simmering the whole hips in a little water until tender. These should then be sieved. Dilute the resulting thick purée with some rosewater; add sugar and lemon juice to taste.

To enjoy the surprisingly exotic flavour and lovely colour of this sauce, serve it with a simple pudding such as junket or blancmange. The latter should be white, as its name indicates.

ROSE HIP SYRUP

1 kg/2 lb ripe rose hips *1½ litres/3 pints water*
sugar *pinch cinnamon (optional)*

Wash the fruit and remove the calyces. Mince or chop the fruit coarsely and pour over 1½-litres (3-pints) boiling water. Bring the mixture to the boil and simmer for 15 minutes or until tender. Remove from the heat and leave for 15 minutes. Pour the fruit into a jelly bag and leave to drain overnight.

Measure the juice and add 350 g (12 oz) sugar to every ½-litre (1-pint). Heat together, stirring until the sugar is dissolved. Pour the syrup into warmed bottles with screw lids. Sterilize in simmering water for 20 minutes. Remove carefully and tighten the lids.

The syrup keeps well sealed but once opened should be kept in the refrigerator. It can be used as a sauce for a steamed pudding, or try a tablespoon diluted with soda water or added to a milk shake for a tempting drink.

ELDERBERRY AND CRAB-APPLE JELLY

450 g/1 lb crab-apples *1 kg/2½ lb elderberries*
½ litre/1 pint water *sugar*
lemon juice

Roughly chop the apples and put in a saucepan with the elderberries and water. Cover and simmer until soft. Strain the fruit through a jellybag. Measure the juice and to each ½ litre (1 pint) add 450 g (1 lb) sugar, and the juice of one lemon. Place over a low heat and stir until the sugar has dissolved. Boil rapidly until set. Pour into warm jars and tie down.

This produces jelly of a beautiful colour which can be used for sweets or as an accompaniment to meat. To garnish a platter of cold meats, fill peach halves with a spoonful of jelly and arrange down the centre of the dish.

SPICED BRAMBLE JELLY

450 g/1 lb blackberries
150 ml/¼ pint cider vinegar
450 g/1 lb soft brown sugar

150 ml/¼ pint water
2 cloves
3 cm/1 inch stick cinnamon

Simmer the fruit in water with the spices until tender. Press through a sieve and return to a clean pan. Add the vinegar and sugar and stir until dissolved. Boil until setting point is reached, about 20 minutes. Pour into small warm pots and seal.

Use to accompany meat or game.

BLACKBERRY AND APPLE JAM

1½ kg/3 lb blackberries
2¾ kg/6 lb sugar
2 lemons

1¾ kg/4 lb apples
575 ml/1 pint water

Peel, core and slice the apples. Place them in a preserving pan with the water and simmer gently until soft. Add the blackberries and cook for a further 5–10 minutes until cooked. Stir in the warmed sugar and juice from the lemons. Boil rapidly until the jam is set. Pot and tie down in the usual way.

SEEDLESS BLACKBERRY AND APPLE JAM

1¾ kg/4 lb blackberries
2¾ kg/6 lb sugar
2 lemons

1¾ kg/4 lb apples
575 ml/1 pint water

Peel, core and slice the apples and simmer in 275 ml (½ pint) water. Place the blackberries in a separate pan and simmer in remaining water until tender; sieve to remove the seeds and add the pulp to the apples. Continue as in recipe above.

This variation is included because many people, particularly the elderly, find blackberries very trying to eat because of their pips.

BLACKBERRY CURD

450 g/1 lb blackberries
350 g/12 oz butter
1 lemon

225 g/8 oz cooking apples
450 g/1 lb sugar
4 eggs

Peel, core and roughly chop the apples. Place in an ovenproof dish with the blackberries. Put in a low oven until the juices run and the fruit is cooked. Sieve the fruit, add lemon juice and put in a double saucepan together with the butter and sugar. Heat gently, stirring, until the sugar is dissolved. Lightly beat the eggs and strain into the fruit mixture. Heat, stirring continuously, until the mixture thickens. Pour into warm jars and seal in the usual way for jam.

All fruit curds made with eggs have a limited keeping life and should be used within one month. Alternatively, they can be frozen satisfactorily for up to three months.

Use like lemon curd for tart fillings, cake filling, with ice cream or as a spread.

ROWAN JELLY

1.4 kg/3 lb ripe red
   rowanberries
water

675 g/1½ lb crab-apples
sugar

Wash the berries and pick out any dried or shrivelled ones. Remove them from their stalks with a large-pronged fork. Roughly chop the crab-apples and place in a preserving pan with the berries. Just cover with water, and simmer until soft. Leave to drain through a jellybag overnight. To each half litre (1 pint) of juice add 350 g (12 oz) sugar. Bring slowly to the boil, stirring until the sugar is dissolved. Boil rapidly until a little jelly on a saucer wrinkles when pushed with a spoon. Pour into clean warm jars and seal as usual.

This jelly has a tart, smoky flavour and is excellent as an accompaniment to cold meat or game instead of redcurrant jelly.

BLACK JAM

1 kg/2 lb blackberries *1 kg/2½ lb elderberries*
1.4 kg/3 lb sugar *½ litre/1 pint water*
juice of 1 lemon

Strip the elderberries from their stalks by using the prongs of a large table fork. Wash the fruit in a colander, carefully removing any debris. Place in a preserving pan with water and simmer until soft. Sieve and return to the pan. Add the blackberries and simmer until cooked for about 10 minutes. Warm the sugar in the oven and add with the lemon juice to the fruit mixture. Stir until dissolved and boil rapidly until setting point is reached. Pour into warm dry jars and seal as usual.

ELDER ROB

FOR COUGHS AND COLDS

ripe elderberries *demerara sugar*
cloves *root ginger*

Place the prepared fruit in an ovenproof dish and crush well to extract the juice. Put in a slow oven and cook for 45 minutes. Strain through muslin or a fine nylon sieve.

To each ½ litre (1 pint) of juice add: 450 g (1 lb) demerara; a piece of root ginger well bruised, and 4 cloves tied in muslin. Stir until the sugar is dissolved and simmer for 30 minutes; remove the spices after 15 minutes. Strain and bottle when cold.

To use as a hot drink, dilute one tablespoon in a glass of hot water. As a soothing mixture for coughs, dilute 2 tablespoons Elder Rob with 1 tablespoon honey in a glass of hot water.

BRAMBLE CORDIAL

1 kg/2 lb ripe blackberries
225 g/8 oz sugar
225 g/8 oz honey

275 ml/½ pint cider vinegar
8 cloves
25 g/1 oz root ginger

Put the fruit in a large bowl and crush well. Pour over boiling vinegar. Leave for three days, stirring each day with a wooden spoon.

Strain into an enamel or aluminium saucepan and add the sugar and honey. Bruise the ginger and tie in muslin with the cloves. Add this to the juice and bring to the boil, stirring to dissolve sugar. Simmer for 15 minutes. Remove the spices and allow the juice to cool. Bottle and store in a dark place or the light will fade the cordial.

Use diluted with hot water for a soothing winter drink or serve with soda water in summer.

RASPBERRY VINEGAR

1 kg/2 lb raspberries
sugar

1 litre/2 pints red wine vinegar

Place the fruit in a bowl. Crush lightly and pour over the vinegar. Cover. Leave for a week, stirring every day.

Strain the fruit through a jellybag and measure the liquid. Allow ½ kg (1 lb) sugar to each ½ litre (1 pint) of juice and place together in a preserving pan. Stir over low heat until the sugar is dissolved, then boil for 10 minutes. When cold bottle.

Fruit and herb vinegars would be on the shelves of all well-stocked Victorian larders, and it is strange that such a versatile ingredient should have become almost extinct. They give a most unexpected lift when used as the basis for salad dressings, are good for flavouring sauces and particularly useful for drinks.

In summer add 2–3 tablespoons to a glass of iced soda water; in winter dilute with hot water.

ELDERBERRY CHUTNEY

1 kg/2 lb elderberries
225 g/8 oz onions
½ litre/1 pint vinegar
1 teaspoon salt
½ teaspoon cayenne pepper

¾ kg/1½ lb cooking apples
225 g/8 oz sugar
1 teaspoon pickling spice
1 teaspoon ground ginger

Chop the onions finely and simmer until tender in half the vinegar. Add the elderberries, the peeled and chopped apples, the spices tied together in muslin, and all the remaining ingredients except the sugar. Cover and simmer gently until the apples are cooked. Add the sugar and when dissolved cook without a lid until the chutney is thick, approximately 40 minutes. Remove the pickling spices and pour into hot jars. Cover with synthetic skin.

All chutneys should be kept for 6–8 weeks to mature.

BLACKBERRY KETCHUP

1½ kg/3 lb blackberries
275 ml/½ pint water
1 tablespoon pickling spices

sugar, soft brown
cider vinegar
salt

Simmer the blackberries in water until tender. Sieve. Boil one tablespoon pickling spices in ½ litre (1 pint) vinegar. To each ½ litre (1 pint) of fruit purée add 50 g (2 oz) sugar, 275 ml (½ pint) spiced vinegar and 1 teaspoon salt. Simmer together until thick, stirring constantly.

Pour the boiling ketchup into clean, hot jars within 2 cm (¾ inch) of the top and cork. Secure the corks with wire or string to prevent the heat blowing them off during sterilization. Stand the jars on a board or folded cloth in a large pan of hot water and bring to the boil. Simmer very gently for 20 minutes. Remove the jars and leave to cool. When cold, paint round the cork with melted paraffin wax to make an airtight seal.

Store in a dark cupboard and keep for at least one month before use.

Ketchups are traditionally offered with cold meats. Try adding a small amount to a curry sauce or beef stew as the fruit and spice content give an extra richness and flavour.

ELDERBERRY WINE

MAKES SIX BOTTLES

1½ kg/3 lb elderberries
1 Campden tablet dissolved
  in 2 tablespoons warm water
1¼ g/2¾ lb granulated sugar

1 teaspoon yeast nutrient
4½ litres/1 gallon water
1 teaspoon wine yeast

Strip the berries from the stalks by using the prongs of a large table fork. Wash well under running water and pick out any remaining debris and shrivelled berries. Place the fruit in a plastic bucket or other suitable fermenting container and crush well. Pour on boiling water. Allow to cool to 70° F (35° C) before adding the dissolved Campden tablet. Cover with a thick cloth or plastic secured with elastic and leave for 24 hours.

Stir in the yeast and yeast nutrient and leave for 4 days; stir daily with a wooden spoon and keep the container covered.

Strain the liquid onto sugar and stir until dissolved. Pour into sterilized 4½-litre (1-gallon) jar, topping up with boiled water if necessary. Plug with cotton-wool initially as elderberries produce a startlingly vigorous ferment. After a day or so fit a fermentation lock and keep in a dark place until fermentation is complete.

Rack (siphon) into a clean jar leaving behind every trace of sediment. Leave for 2–3 months to clear and rack again. The wine can be bottled at this stage but the flavour is improved if it matures in bulk; it should be left for at least a year. Keep in dark bottles or a dark cupboard to prevent the colour fading.

The elderberry fruits lavishly each year and it is worth gathering as many berries as possible in order to freeze them. Choose a fine warm day for the expedition; on returning strip the berries from the stalks and freeze immediately in suitable quantities for future use. Elderberries also make excellent wine when combined with apples, blackberries or any of the wild plums.

ROWANBERRY WINE

MAKES SIX BOTTLES

1½ kg/3 lb rowanberries　　*450 g/1 lb raisins*
1¼ kg/2½ lb sugar　　　　*4½ litres/1 gallon water*
1 teaspoon each of citric acid,
　yeast and yeast nutrient

Wash the berries and remove the stalks. Place the fruit in a large plastic or earthenware container and pour boiling water over it. Cover and leave for 4 days, stirring daily with a wooden spoon.

Strain and return the juice to a clean container. Add sugar, chopped raisins and citric acid and stir until the sugar is dissolved. Cover closely and keep in a warm place for 2 weeks.

Strain into a fermenting jar and fit an air-lock. When the liquid clears, rack and bottle as usual. Allow to mature for at least six months before use.

This makes a very good dry table wine.

NUTS

The only native of these four important nut-bearing trees is the hazel. It grows luxuriantly in hedgerows throughout Britain and can produce a harvest of commercial proportions. The walnut, sweet chestnut and almond come from warmer climates of southern Europe and South-East Asia and their origins are reflected in their unpredictable crops here. To ensure a good nut harvest it is necessary to have a hot summer and a dry autumn. However, even in our fickle climate nuts are rewarding to search for and find as a mere handful of them can create or transform a dish.

The almond and the chestnut were probably introduced into Britain by the Romans, and the walnut followed some five hundred years later. Although not strictly hedgerow trees, they flourish in many parts of the country. When found they will probably be escapes from cultivation although Gerard writing in 1592 mentions walnut trees as being frequently seen in fields near common highways.

Walnuts are prized where ever they are grown which is reflected in their name Jove's or Jupiter's Nut. They were the food of the gods when mortals lived on acorns. Like the hazel nut in Celtic lore, the walnut was valued as a fertility symbol. It was scattered at Roman weddings for the same purpose that we still throw rice, and when the tree was introduced into England its magical properties were perpetuated here. In East Anglia walnut shells have been found under the floorboards of Tudor rooms where they served the dual purpose of encouraging procreation and protecting the house from evil spirits.

Nuts were very useful in divining the future and in some areas the festival of All Hallows' E'en had the alternative title of Nut-crack Day. The nuts would be thrown into the fire as a silent wish was made; the wish would be granted if the nut blazed, but a quiet smouldering indicated that the spirits would not be co-operating. A variation of the plum stone formula was to place nuts in the fire with the request:

> If he loves me pop and fly
> If he hates me lie and die.

Deviation from normal growth in nature is usually associated with magical powers. Anyone who found two kernels in one nut would be considered to have a very lucky talisman; the correct procedure was to eat one and throw the other over the head in the sure expectation that a wish would be granted.

From the earliest times the indigenous hazel was considered the Tree of Knowledge. It was therefore a quite logical deduction for the Celts to assume that the nut itself contained the kernel of wisdom. It was accepted that trout which had fed on the nuts would pass on great knowledge to those who in turn ate them; readers may consider this fact alone is sufficient recommendation for the hazelnut stuffing for fish recipe. The powers of the hazel can also be transmitted by using her twigs to divine for water, as a protection against evil spirits or to charm away warts. And if further proof is needed, it was a hazel branch that enabled St Patrick to drive the snakes out of Ireland.

The use of the hazelnut as a delicate flavouring in cakes and puddings is a sophisticated and comparatively recent development; it came from the Continent where nuts are extensively grown as a crop and much appreciated in the kitchen. Formerly the English countryman gained his enjoyment of the wild nuts as much from the gathering of the crop as from the eating. Nutting was a family occasion and eagerly looked forward to. Until the First World War, many village schools closed on Holy Cross day, 14th September, and the children traditionally spent the holiday nutting. This was before the explosion in the grey squirrel population which today tends to consume the crop before it is ripe.

ALMOND SOUP

SERVES SIX

50 g/2 oz almonds
1 onion
25 g/1 oz flour
2 egg yolks

1 white stick of celery
850 ml/1½ pints milk
25 g/1 oz butter
few toasted split almonds

Blanch and chop the almonds. Simmer in milk with a whole onion and a celery stick for 20 minutes. Cover and leave to infuse for a further 10 minutes. Discard the vegetables and place the soup in a liquidizer with butter and flour. Blend and return to the saucepan. Simmer, stirring, for 5 minutes until the flour is thoroughly cooked. Season. Beat the egg yolks and whisk into the hot soup.

Serve immediately with a scattering of toasted almonds on each portion.

Almond Soup has delicate flavour and Royal patronage; it was served at the English and French Courts from the Middle Ages.

CHESTNUT SOUP

SERVES SIX

½ kg/1½ lbs chestnuts
1 carrot
850 ml/1½ pints game stock
croutons

1 small onion
1 stick celery
salt, pepper
1 glass Madeira

Put the chestnuts into a pan of cold water and bring to the boil. Boil for 10 minutes. Take out two or three nuts at a time in order to remove the inner and outer skins. As the water cools and the skins become difficult to peel, reheat to boiling again. Put the peeled nuts in a clean saucepan with the stock, chopped onion and chopped celery. Bring slowly to the boil, cover and simmer until the nuts are soft. Liquidize. Add the Madeira and check the seasoning. Reheat and serve with croutons.

A complete contrast to the preceding recipe, Chestnut Soup is rich and substantial and reflects its northern origins.

Dried Chestnuts. Our climate does not normally allow the nuts to grow to a worthwhile size for drying supplies for winter use. In order to extend the chestnut season, excellent results can be obtained using tinned chestnut purée for desserts, or dried chestnuts for the recipes given for soup, stuffings and brussels sprouts; both are available from good delicatessens.

CHESTNUTS AND BRUSSEL SPROUTS

Cook the chestnuts and brussels sprouts separately in the proportion of 225 g (8 oz) peeled nuts to 450 g (1 lb) sprouts. Drain and toss together in butter and seasoning.

This robust combination can accompany the main course at any winter meal and is sufficiently substantial not to require potatoes as well.

CHESTNUTS AND TURKEY

For a stuffing
450 g/1 lb cooked chestnuts   *2 rashers bacon*
1 onion   *little milk or stock*
1 tablespoon fresh herbs   *salt and pepper*

Dice the bacon and fry with the chopped onion. Mash the chestnuts and mix in the bacon, onion and seasoning. Moisten with a
little milk or stock and use to stuff the breast of turkey.

Or Core small cooking apples and fill them with the above
     mixture. Roast in a tin round the bird for the last hour of
     cooking.

Or If not making chestnut stuffing, add 125 g (¼ lb) puréed
     chestnuts to the gravy. This will enrich and thicken it.

HAZELNUT STUFFING

TO SERVE WITH FISH

125 g/4 oz fresh breadcrumbs   *2 shallots*
50 g/2 oz hazelnuts   *2 tablespoons fresh herbs*
1 egg   *(parsley, thyme)*
1 lemon   *salt, pepper*
a little milk for mixing

Chop the nuts coarsley and chop the shallots finely; add both to the
breadcrumbs, grated lemon rind and finely milled fresh herbs. Stir
in the lemon juice, beaten egg and enough milk to give a firm
consistency. Season well.

Use to stuff fresh haddock or an oversize trout which has lost the
delicate flavour of youth; these latter can be bought at intensive
fish rearing farms.

WALNUT AND APRICOT STUFFING

50 g/2 oz dried apricots
125 g/4 oz fresh breadcrumbs
50 g/2 oz coarsely chopped
  walnuts

2 tablespoons finely milled parsley
grated rind and juice of 1 orange
1 egg

Cover the apricots with water and leave to soak overnight. Drain and chop the apricots, retaining the liquid. Mix all the dry ingredients together and bind with beaten egg and orange juice; use the liquid from the apricots to moisten the stuffing if it is too dry.

The texture of the nuts combined with the slightly sharp fruit is unexpected in this unusual Australian recipe.

This stuffing is particularly good with lamb for which you require a boned shoulder. Place the stuffing in the cavity in the centre of the shoulder and tie the roast securely with string. Weigh the stuffed joint and place in a baking tin in preheated oven (350° F, 180° C or Gas no. 4). Allow 30 minutes to each 450 g (1 lb) plus 15 minutes for the roast to rest before carving.

WALDORF SALAD

4 firm red-skinned apples
  (e.g. Worcester Pearmain)
175 g/6 oz diced celery
125 g/4 oz chopped walnuts

lettuce
2 tablespoons lemon juice
150 ml/¼ pint mayonnaise

Core the apples but do not peel them as the skin colour adds to the attractive appearance of the salad. Chop them coarsely into the lemon juice mixed with 275 ml (½ pint) water which will prevent discoloration. Drain and toss together with the celery, walnuts and mayonnaise. Place on a bed of lettuce and serve at once.

As suggested by its name, this deliciously crunchy salad is an American importation. American salads are characterized by their imaginative use of fruit and nuts together with the more conventional ingredients. The addition of 50 g (2 oz) of chopped dates is a pleasant variation.

Waldorf Salad is particularly good with cold game birds or turkey and should be accompanied by potatoes baked in their jackets.

SAVOURY NUT PIE

SERVES FOUR TO SIX

450 g/1 lb potatoes	*milk*
175 g/6 oz coarsely chopped mixed nuts	*2 tablespoons finely milled parsley*
1 onion	*1 teaspoon fresh thyme*
50 g/2 oz mushrooms	*50 g/2 oz butter*

Boil the potatoes and mash to a purée with the milk, seasoning and a little butter. Slice the onion and sauté in butter until transparent. Add the chopped mushrooms and fry for a further minute or so. Mix into the mashed potatoes together with the nuts, thyme and parsley. Bind with a little milk if too dry and place in well greased pie dish. Sprinkle the top with breadcrumbs and parsley and dot with butter. Bake at 350° F (180° C or Gas no. 4) for 20 minutes.

PICKLED WALNUTS

Walnuts for pickling should be picked in late June before the shell starts to harden as after that no amount of soaking will soften it. Prick the bottom of each nut with a pin to ensure that it is completely soft. Rubber gloves are essential as the walnut stain is virtually impossible to remove.

green walnuts
½ litre/1 pint vinegar
10 g/½ oz root ginger

1 tablespoon pickling spice
brine (made up from 75 g/3 oz
*   salt to ½ litre/1 pint water)*

Prick each walnut deeply several times with a fork. Soak them in brine for 4 days. Drain and cover with fresh brine for a further 4 days.

Drain and place the nuts on a tray in a sunny window. Turn them occasionally. Depending on the weather the exposure to the air will gradually turn the nuts black—usually a matter of 2–3 days.

Boil the well-bruised ginger and pickling spice in vinegar for 10 minutes. Strain and allow to cool.

Pack the blackened walnuts into jars. Pour over the cold spiced vinegar.

Tie down and leave to mature for 2 months.

SWEET PICKLED WALNUTS

green walnuts
½ litre/1 pint wine vingar
3 shallots
10 g/½ root ginger

1 tablespoon mixed pickling spice
225 g/8 oz soft brown sugar
1 lemon

Follow the method above for preparing and drying the walnuts.

Place all the ingredients except the lemon in a saucepan and boil for 10 minutes. Cool.

Place a slice of lemon at the bottom of each jar; pack with the blackened walnuts and cover with cold spiced vinegar.

Tie down and keep for 2 months before use.

Pickled walnuts are traditionally eaten with bread and cheese. Any liquor remaining in the jars after the nuts have been eaten can be used as the base for making a piquant sauce or relish.

ITALIAN CREAM ICE

SERVES FOUR

1 egg white
25 g/1 oz almonds
2 tablespoons brandy

150 ml/¼ pint double cream
2 tablespoons sifted icing sugar

Split the almonds and toast them until they are lightly coloured.

Whisk the cream until it falls softly from the beater; add the sifted icing sugar and continue whipping until thick.

In a separate basin, whisk the egg white until stiff and fold into the cream together with the brandy. Put into individual souflée dishes and sprinkle with almonds. Freeze until firm.

Two hours before the meal, take the dishes from the freezer and place in the refrigerator to ripen. The ice should be semi-frozen when eaten.

MARRONS GLACÉ

1 kg/2 lb chestnuts
½ litre/1 pint water

½ kg/1½ lb sugar
1 vanilla pod

Remove the outer skin from the chestnuts. Put them in a large pan of boiling water and simmer for 25 minutes until tender. Peel.

To make the syrup, dissolve the sugar in ½ litre (1 pint) water; bring to the boil and simmer for 5 minutes. Add the peeled chestnuts and vanilla pod and simmer for a further 5 minutes. Leave for 24 hours.

Next day bring the syrup and the nuts to the boil; remove from the heat and leave to cool.

Repeat on the third day. Remove the chestnuts with a slotted spoon to a cake rack to drain and dry. Place them in petits-fours paper cases if for immediate consumption, or wrap individually in foil if required to keep.

Use the syrup for ice cream, sweet sauces or for apple compote.

CHESTNUT PAVLOVA

SERVES SIX

*1 18-cm (7-inch) meringue
case
275 ml/½ pint double cream
1 tablespoon grated chocolate*

*2 egg whites
225 g/½ lb sweetened chestnut
purée
1 tablespoon rum*

Whisk the egg whites until they are stiff. Whip the cream until it hangs loosely from the beater. Fold the chestnut purée into the cream. Add the egg whites and blend carefully together. Pile onto the meringue case and decorate with grated chocolate.

Make several hours before required to allow the meringue to soften; serve chilled.

HAZELNUT CREAM (BAVAROISE)

SERVES FOUR TO SIX

*3 egg yolks
2–3 drops vanilla essence
50 g/2 oz castor sugar
150 g/5 oz hazelnuts*

*425 ml/¾ pint milk
150 ml/¼ pint double cream
10 g/½ oz gelatine*

Toast the nuts in the oven for 5 minutes until they are light brown; remove and rub off the skins. Reserve a few for decoration and grind or pound finely the remainder.

Make a custard in the usual way by heating milk and pouring it onto beaten eggs and sugar. Return to the pan and stir over a low heat until thick. Add vanilla essence. Strain and set aside to cool.

Sprinkle the gelatine into 3 tablespoons cold water and leave for a few minutes to soak. Dissolve over hot water until clear, and stir into the custard. Add the ground hazelnuts, 2 tablespoons of the cream and mix in well. Pour into an oiled mould or serving dish and chill.

Garnish with whipped cream and decorate with whole nuts.

Under the name Bavaroise, this classic Continental pudding has appeared on all the best menus for the past hundred years. The flavouring can be chocolate, coffee or vanilla, but hazelnut is the most delicate.

MONT BLANC

VERY RICH; SERVES SIX TO EIGHT

1 kg/2 lbs chestnuts
vanilla pod
2 tablespoons icing sugar

½ litre/1 pint milk
275 ml/½ pint double cream
1 tablespoon brandy or rum

Boil and remove the chestnut skins—see Chestnut Soup (page 76) for details of the method. Cook the nuts in a double boiler with the milk and vanilla pod. When the mixture is the consistency of porridge, remove the vanilla and put the mixture through a ricer, or mouli-sieve, straight onto the serving dish as a central mound.

Whip the cream and fold in the sugar and liquor. Pour this on top of the sieved chestnut and serve well chilled.

BANANA AND WALNUT PUDDING

SERVES THREE TO FOUR

3 small trifle sponges
3 tablespoons demerara sugar
1 orange
275 ml/½ pint milk
1 tablespoon rum

2 bananas
25 g/1 oz walnuts
¼ teaspoon nutmeg
1 egg

Crumble the sponge cakes and place half in the bottom of a 1-litre (2-pint) greased oven dish. Cover with sliced bananas. Chop the nuts and mix with the grated orange peel, sugar and nutmeg and spread this over the bananas. Add the remaining cake and sprinkle the orange juice on top. Warm the milk and add this to the lightly whisked egg and rum and pour mixture over pudding. Bake at 350° F (180° C or Gas no. 4) for 35 minutes. Serve hot.

AMERICAN CUSTARD TART

SERVES FOUR

225 g/8 oz shortcrust pastry   *3 eggs*
425 ml/¾ pint milk   *75 g/3 oz castor sugar*
125 g/4 oz mixed nuts   *cinnamon*

Place a baking sheet in the oven and set to 400° F (200° C or Gas no. 6). Line a 20-cm (8-inch) flan ring with the pastry, prick the base with a fork and place in the refrigerator while preparing the filling.

Heat the milk almost to boiling point and pour onto the beaten eggs and sugar. Stir well and strain. Add the finely chopped nuts and pour carefully into the pastry case. Dust with cinnamon. Place on the baking sheet in the hot oven and bake for approximately 30 minutes until the custard is set.

Sprinkle the tart with castor sugar and serve warm.

The nuts rise to the top of the custard filling and give this tart a most unusual and delicious flavour.

PRALINE

equal quantities of unblanched almonds and castor sugar

Put the sugar into a heavy saucepan over low heat until it is melted. Add the roughly chopped almonds and cook, stirring with a metal spoon until the nuts are well toasted and the mixture is a good brown. Pour into an oiled tin and leave to cool.

When cold, break up and reduce to a coarse powder in the blender or with a rolling pin between two sheets of strong brown paper.

Store in an airtight screwtop jar. Use to flavour ice-cream, gâteaux, puddings and soufflées.

Coffee and nuts are an irresistible combination. Make a cold coffee soufflé and fold in 2 tablespoons praline with the stiffly beaten egg whites. When set decorate with whipped cream and praline scattered on top.

BUTTERCREAM PRALINE FILLING

TO SERVE WITH MERINGUES

125 g/4 oz unsalted butter　　*1 egg yolk*
225 g/½ lb icing sugar　　*1 teaspoon orangeflower water*
1 tablespoon brandy　　*1 tablespoon praline (see opposite)*

Cream the butter until it is light and fluffy. Beat in the sifted icing sugar and praline alternately with the egg yolk and liquids until all the ingredients are well blended.

Sandwich the meringue shells together with this filling and decorate with a sprinkling of chopped nuts down each centre.

WEST INDIAN WALNUT SLICES

MAKES EIGHT

75 g/3 oz butter　　*2 tablespoons melted black treacle*
75 g/3 oz soft brown sugar　　*1 egg*
1 tablespoon chopped　　*125 g/4 oz self-raising flour*
*   walnuts*　　*1 teaspoon baking powder*
　　a little milk

Grease and line an 18-cm (7-inch) square tin. Beat the butter and sugar together until light; beat in the warmed treacle. Sift the flour and baking powder together and add to the creamed mixture alternately with the lightly beaten egg. Fold in the chopped nuts and turn into the prepared tin. Bake in a preheated moderate oven (350° F, 180° C or Gas no. 4) for approximately 30 minutes. Turn onto a wire rack and leave till cold.

For the Icing
　125 g/4 oz icing sugar　　*1 teaspoon instant coffee*
　walnuts to decorate

Sift together the icing sugar and instant coffee. Mix with about 3–4 teaspoons boiling water and spread over the cake. Decorate with whole nuts and cut into slices.

CREOLE KISSES

MAKES EIGHTEEN

225 g/8 oz icing sugar   *3 egg whites*
2 tablespoons flour   *125 g/4 oz walnuts*

Grease and line thoroughly two baking trays. Grind or chop the walnuts finely. Sift together the flour and icing sugar into a large mixing bowl. Whisk the egg whites until stiff and fold them gently into the flour, together with the nuts. Put dessertspoonfuls of the mixture well apart on the prepared trays. Bake in a preheated moderate oven (350° F, 180° C or Gas no. 4) for approximately 20 minutes until they have risen and are pale biscuit coloured. Handle carefully as they are fragile when warm. Cool on a wire tray and store in an airtight tin.

These featherlight biscuits are delicious served with coffee or to accompany a special pudding. For such occasions make smaller ones by using a teaspoon to measure out the mixture.

HAZELNUT MERINGUES

MAKES TEN TO TWELVE MERINGUES

2 egg whites   *50 g/2 oz hazelnuts*
125 g/4 oz castor sugar

Roast the hazelnuts in the oven for 5 minutes until they are light brown. Turn onto a cloth and rub over briskly to remove any skins or fibres. Chop the nuts finely.

Whisk the egg whites until they stand up in peaks. Add 1 tablespoon of sugar and whisk again until as stiff as before. Gently fold in the remaining sugar and the prepared nuts. Place tablespoons of the mixture onto oiled greaseproof paper, on a baking tray. Bake in preheated oven (250° F, 130° C or Gas no. ½) for approximately 2 hours and until the meringues are thoroughly dry. They will peel cleanly away from the paper when done.

When cold, store in an airtight container until required.

ALMOND CRESCENTS

MAKES ABOUT SIXTY

225 g/8 oz self-raising flour
25 g/1 oz cocoa
125 g/4 oz butter
chopped almonds

50 g/2 oz ground almonds
125 g/4 oz castor sugar
1 egg plus 1 egg white

Sieve together the flour and cocoa and rub in the butter until the mixture resembles fine breadcumbs. Add the sugar and ground almonds. Mix to form a dough with the lightly beaten egg and knead until smooth. Roll out thinly and cut into crescents using a round cutter. Place on a greased baking tin. Brush over with lightly beaten egg white and sprinkle with chopped almonds. Bake in a preheated oven (375° F, 190° C or Gas no. 5) for 10–15 minutes.

Cool on a wire rack and store in an airtight tin.

WALNUT BROWNIES

MAKES TWELVE

50 g/2 oz white vegetable fat
1 egg
125 g/4 oz plain flour
½ teaspoon salt

200 g/7 oz soft brown sugar
50 g/2 oz walnuts
1 teaspoon baking powder
½ teaspoon vanilla essence

Grease and line a 20-cm (8-inch) square and 2-cm (½-inch) deep cake tin. Melt the fat over a low heat and stir in the sugar. When cool, add the well beaten egg. Sift the flour, baking powder and salt together and stir into the fat and sugar mixture. Add the vanilla essence and the chopped walnuts. Mix well and turn into a prepared tin. Bake in a preheated oven (350° F, 180° C or Gas no. 4) for about 20 minutes.

Leave to cool in the tin and cut into squares when cold.

ALMOND CAKE

225 g/8 oz butter	*225 g/8 oz castor sugar*
175 g/6 oz self-raising flour	*75 g/3 oz ground almonds*
4 large eggs	*almond essence*
flaked almonds for decoration	*pinch salt*

Grease thoroughly a 20-cm (8-inch) cake tin.

Sift together the flour and salt. Beat the eggs lightly. Cream the butter and sugar until light and fluffy. Beat in the eggs a little at a time, adding some of the sieved flour if the mixture looks like separating. Add the ground almonds, 2–3 drops of almond essence and mix thoroughly together before turning into the prepared tin. Sprinkle the flaked almonds over the top and bake in preheated moderate oven (330° F, 170° C or Gas no. 3) for approximately 1½ hours.

Leave in the tin for a few minutes before turning out onto a wire rack to cool.

Because of the ground almonds in the mixture, this is an excellent keeper and can be made a week or two before required.

BANANA AND WALNUT LOAF

225 g/8 oz self-raising flour	*50 g/2 oz butter*
50 g/2 oz sugar	*75 g/3 oz honey*
450 g/1 lb ripe bananas	*2 eggs*
50 g/2 oz chopped walnuts	*½ teaspoon salt*

Grease a 1-kilo (2-lb) loaf tin.

Sift together the flour and salt. Cream the butter and sugar and beat in the honey and lightly beaten eggs. Stir in the mashed bananas, chopped nuts and flour. Mix well. Spoon into the tin and bake at 350° F (180° C or Gas no. 4) for 1¼ hours. Cool on a wire tray.

Serve sliced and buttered. This bread keeps well and can be made a week in advance of requirement.

HAZELNUT CAKE

125 g/4 oz hazelnuts
2 tablespoons dry bread-
  crumbs
½ teaspoon instant coffee

3 eggs
75 g/3 oz icing sugar
1 teaspoon cocoa

Grease and line a 22-cm (9-inch) cake tin.

Sift the icing sugar into a basin, add the egg yolks and beat until thick and white, for approximately 10 to 15 minutes. Sift together the cocoa and coffee and stir into the mixture. Whisk the egg whites until stiff and fold in carefully. Add the grated nuts and the breadcrumbs and mix well. Bake in a preheated moderate oven (350° F, 180° C or Gas no. 4) for approximately 30 minutes. Cool on a wire tray and cover with coffee glacé icing when cold.

To serve for a dinner party: instead of icing, cover the cake with sweetened whipped cream flavoured with brandy.

MACAROONS

225 g/8 oz almonds
2 egg whites
rice paper

175 g/6 oz castor sugar
1 tablespoon cornflour or arrowroot
vanilla essence

Blanch the almonds by plunging into boiling water. Leave in a covered pan for a few minutes before draining and rinsing in cold water. The brown skin should then peel away easily. Rinse and dry thoroughly. Reserve 12 almonds and grind or pound the remainder to fine crumbs.

Mix the sugar and egg whites with the ground almonds until well blended. Stir in the flour and 2–3 drops vanilla essence. Line a baking sheet with rice paper and put spoonfuls of the mixture on it. (If no rice paper is available, use a greased, floured baking sheet.) Press a split almond on each biscuit and bake in a preheated oven (375° F, 190° C or Gas no. 5) for about 20 minutes or until lightly browned.

Cut the rice paper round each macaroon and cool on a wire tray.

WHITE WALNUT CAKE

125 g/4 oz butter	*125 g/4 oz castor sugar*
25 g/1 oz cornflour	*125 g/4 oz self-raising flour*
3 eggs	*1 tablespoon chopped walnuts*
pinch salt	*vanilla essence*

Grease and flour two 16-cm (6-inch) cake tins.

Cream together the butter and sugar until light. Sift together the flours and salt, and lightly whisk the eggs. Gradually beat the eggs into the fat mixture adding a little flour if it tends to curdle. Fold in gently the remaining flour and chopped nuts and mix well together. Divide between tins and bake in the centre of a pre-heated moderate oven (350° F, 180° C or Gas no. 4) for 30 minutes.

Remove from the oven and leave for a few minutes before turning onto a wire rack to cool.

For the filling

75 g/3 oz icing sugar	*30 g/1½ oz butter*
10 g/½ oz walnuts	*vanilla essence*

Cream together the butter, the finely ground nuts and the sifted icing sugar. Add 1–2 drops vanilla essence and use to sandwich the cake when quite cold.

For the icing

The cake can be finished by covering with *glacé icing*. Use 225 g (8 oz) sifted icing sugar mixed with a little boiling water. Spread over the cake and decorate with several half walnuts.

Mountain Icing is the traditional covering for walnut cake but it is a little trickier to make.

225 g/8 oz castor sugar	*½ gill water*
2 egg whites	*pinch cream of tartar*
7 walnut halves	

Heat the sugar in water very gently until dissolved. Raise the heat and boil the syrup without stirring until 240° F (120° C) is reached. Whisk the egg whites until very stiff.

Pour the syrup steadily and gently onto the egg whites, continuing to beat them. This requires either an assistant or an electric mixer to accomplish. Continue whipping until the mixture thickens and holds its shape. Pour immediately over the cake and spread quickly over the top and sides. Press in the walnut halves and leave to set.

There is no greater give-away than the memories evoked by this cake. Depending on one's age, White Walnut Cake is synonymous with Fuller's, the 'thirties and afternoon tea with great aunts.

APPLES AND PLUMS

Crab apples, our small native fruit, were featured in Celtic life and legends, invoked in the Coronation blessing of Saxon kings, and one thousand years later are still a sought-after ingredient for many favourite recipes. The crab is found throughout Britain but has been crossed with imported varieties of apple for many centuries. In addition to deliberate hybridizing, hedgerows have gained apple trees from the farmers' habit of spreading residue from cider presses onto their fields. The hedgerow apple is therefore infinitely variable in colour, size and sweetness and recipes should be adapted accordingly.

Fresh spring water for drinking has always been strictly limited to the small number of people living within easy reach of a source. Before the arrival of fluoridated, recycled, piped drinking water, most of the population depended on the even more dubious qualities provided by the local well. This known health hazard meant that most country households brewed vast quantities of their own ale and made a variety of wines, cordials and vinegars from any fruit and flowers available. Apples were one of the main ingredients and it is not surprising that the trees featured in many ceremonies. The gods had to be wooed, to encourage fertility and to ensure a good harvest, and duly thanked when it had been gathered. In some parts of the country the last apple of the year's crop would be left for the Apple Tree man; he lived in the oldest tree and was responsible for the fruitfulness of the orchard. The custom of Wassailing the trees on Christmas Eve, New Year's Eve or Twelfth Night took place in all apple-growing areas until comparatively recently, and has even been revived in Somerset. In a single noisy ceremony, the farmer and his men would banish the evil spirits with a fusillade of shots, sing prescribed thanksgiving songs, and drink to the health of the gods who controlled the future harvest.

The improbably named, but delicious drink, Lambs Wool, must be one of the oldest recipes still in regular use. At the Celtic festivity of Lugh Long-hand, the sun-god, held on Lammas Day (1st August), the beginning of the harvest would be celebrated with a drink of hot ale containing spices and apples. The original name of this feast day, *La mas nbhal*, gradually transferred itself to the drink and was corrupted to Lambs Wool. Centuries later it became the traditional drink for the eve of All Hallows (All Hallows' E'en) on 31st October.

Halloween customs became so entrenched that some, such as bobbing for apples, still survive masked as party games. The apple played a vital part in the numerous ceremonies concerned with divining the identity of a future wife or husband. Unmarried girls would eat an apple at midnight in a room lit by a single candle; as she looked into the mirror, the image of her husband would appear looking over her left shoulder. A simpler method was merely to place an apple under the pillow on 31st October. However, most charm recipes required added hazards to ensure success; it might be necessary to go upstairs backwards without speaking for three successive Friday nights, for example. In magic much depends on close attention to the detailed ritual demanded. The complications were probably added when it became apparent that simple charms

94

did not always work the first time.

Fire was frequently an important element as an aid to performing a spell. Apple pips placed in front of the fire could be consulted to indicate the fidelity of the current suitor. Plum stones, too, had the power of foretelling the future; the stone would be thrown into the fire with a rhymed instruction and the name of the man. The hoped-for response was for the stone to crack and hurl the kernel out of the fire; it was a very unsatisfactory omen if it merely smouldered away.

Apple trees are normally found growing singly, but the mainstay of the English hedge is the blackthorn. For centuries it has been planted by farmers in order to provide a cheap, quick-growing stockproof hedge. It is most conspicuous in April when its black leafless twigs are covered with the tiny white blossoms which will bring misfortune to anyone foolish enough to wear them or take them into the house. In Hampshire the cold weather which often accompanies the blossom is still called a blackthorn winter, a description recorded by Gilbert White when writing his journal at Selborne in the eighteenth century. The fruit of the blackthorn, the sloe, is used to describe the season in Suffolk where it is referred to as sloe-hatching time. By the autumn the leaves will mask the vicious thorns which guard the small dark-blue fruit; strong gloves together with considerable determination are necessary to pick the sloes in worthwhile quantity.

It is this indigenous shrub which has been crossed to become the ancestor of the bullace, the damson and all our cultivated plums. The bullace has been recognized since the early seventeenth century and only in the last hundred years has it been superseded by better varieties; now it lingers on in many cottage gardens and hedges. It has few, if any, thorns and the variable fruits may be purple, red, green, or yellow. They lack the agonizing acidity of sloes but both sloes and bullace are best picked after the first frost which will remove some of their tartness.

The largest of our hedgerow plums are the damsons. Although unquestionably escaped from cultivation, in the areas where they flourish the fruit is as neglected and unvalued as the bitter sloe.

95

Most of the following recipes are interchangeable depending on the yield of your favourite hedge; because of their stones wild plums are most successful when used in dishes which are sieved or strained, such as jellies and cheese.

APPLE SOUP (HOT)

SAVOURY SOUP FOR SIX

450 g/1 lb cooking apples *1 litre/2 pints beef stock*
½ teaspoon ginger *50 g/2 oz rice, cooked*

Simmer the roughly chopped apples in stock until tender. Sieve or liquidize, and season with ginger and freshly ground black pepper. Add the cooked rice and serve very hot.

APPLE SOUP (COLD)

SWEET SOUP FOR EIGHT

The recipes for apple soup date back many centuries in England and are well worth trying. On the Continent fruit soups have never lost their popularity and are served both hot and cold. This recipe is a Danish one.

¾ kg/1½ lbs cooking apples *2 litres/4 pints water or chicken*
1 cinnamon stick *stock*
25 g/1 oz potato flour *1 lemon*
60 g/2–3 oz sugar *150 ml/¼ pint white wine or cider*

Roughly chop the apples but do not peel them. Put in a large saucepan with 1-litre (2-pints) water, the peeled rind of the lemon and the cinnamon stick. Cover and simmer until the apples are cooked. Remove the cinnamon and lemon rind and purée the apples. Return the apple to the saucepan and add the remaining litre (2-pints) water and the sugar. Mix the potato flour with a little cold water and stir into the soup. Bring slowly to the boil, stirring until the soup thickens. Add the wine and taste for sweetness; it should have a sharp, fresh flavour.

Serve chilled with a swirl of whipped cream on top.

AUTUMN OMELETTE

The everyday ingredients in this simple recipe combine to make an unusual and delicious supper dish. To prevent leather-like results, omelettes are always better when cooked individually and should be served immediately. As they are one of the few egg dishes to be cooked over fast heat it only takes a moment or so to produce each one once the ingredients are assembled.

For each person allow:
2 medium eggs
½ firm dessert apple
salt and pepper

25 g/1 oz butter
1 heaped tablespoon grated cheese

Quarter the apple, peel and cut into thick slices. Heat half the butter in a frying pan and fry the apple slices gently for a few minutes until tender but still firm. Meanwhile heat the remainder of the butter in an omelette pan. Lightly beat eggs and season with salt and freshly ground black pepper. Pour the mixture into the heated pan and, when the base is cooked and set, spread the hot apple slices down the centre of the omelette. Sprinkle on grated cheese and fold smartly in half as you turn the cooked omelette onto a waiting warmed plate.

Serve with thin slices of brown bread and butter and a green salad.

HERRING SURPRISE

SERVES FOUR

4 herrings
225 g/½ lb apples (cooking
or dessert)
50 g/2 oz fresh bread-
crumbs

1 small onion or 3 shallots
1 teaspoon sugar
10 g/½ oz melted butter
salt, pepper

Scale, clean and wash the herrings. Split open and remove the backbone.

Chop the apple and onion finely and mix together with the sugar and all but 1 tablespoon of the breadcrumbs. Season well. Place the stuffing inside each fish and roll up carefully from head to tail. Place in a greased ovenproof dish. Sprinkle over the remainder of the crumbs and pour over melted butter. Bake in a moderate oven (350° F, 180° C or Gas no. 4) for 25 minutes.

FIDGET PIE

SERVES FOUR TO SIX

450 g/1 lb thickly sliced raw
potatoes
450 g/1 lb peeled, cored and
sliced apples

275 ml/½ pint stock
225 g/½ lb bacon or ham diced
brown sugar if apples are sour
175 g/6 oz shortcrust pastry

Layer the potatoes, the apples and the bacon in a pie dish and season. Repeat the layers until the dish is full. Add stock and cover with pastry. Brush with beaten egg and bake for 20 minutes at 400° F (200° C or Gas no. 6); lower heat to 350° F (180° C or Gas no. 4) and bake for a further 45 minutes.

This is a Shropshire recipe but variations on the theme come from many parts of the country with apples being the common ingredient. In Cheshire layers of pork and in the West Country mutton are the meats used.

SAVOURY STUFFED APPLES

SERVES FOUR

Sauté a finely chopped onion in butter. Add a few chopped mushroom stems and cook a little longer. Mix this into 225 g (½ lb) pork sausage meat. Add some fresh herbs and season well.

To use as a garnish for roast pork, duck or goose, fill small apples with this savoury mixture and put in a roasting tin to cook with the meat.

As a light supper dish, allow one large apple per person. Fill each one generously with the sausagemeat and roast in a greased dish for 45 minutes in moderate oven (350° F, 180° C or Gas no. 4).

Quantities given are enough for stuffing four large apples.

SWEET STUFFED APPLES

Bramble Apples

Allow one apple per person. Score each fruit round its middle and take a generous core from the centre. Place in a baking dish and fill the apples with fresh blackberries. Top each with a dessertspoon of soft brown sugar and a knob of butter. Mix two tablespoons honey with 275 ml (½ pint) hot water and pour into a baking dish. Bake at 325° F (170° C or Gas no. 3) for 45 minutes, basting occasionally.

Mincemeat Apples

Mix mincemeat with a tablespoon of brandy or rum and use as stuffing. Follow the recipe above for detail.

Spicy Stuffed Apples

Roughly chop dates and walnuts and mix together with honey and a pinch of cinnamon. Fill the apple centres with this mixture and replace a portion of the core to prevent the stuffing becoming dry. Mix together 2 tablespoons golden syrup with 275 ml (½ pint) cider and pour round the apples. Baste occasionally during cooking.

APPLE KISSEL

SERVES FOUR TO FIVE

450 g/1 lb apples
1 lemon
2 tablespoons potato flour
damson cheese for garnish

½ litre/1 pint water
125 g/4 oz sugar
3 tablespoons white wine
  (optional)

Chop the apples and cook in water over a low heat until tender.
Sieve. Return to a clean pan with the grated lemon rind, the lemon
juice and the sugar. Bring to the boil, stirring until the sugar is
dissolved. Mix the potato flour with 3 tablespoons white wine (or
water) and stir into the hot purée. Cook, stirring, until it clears
and thickens.

For extra elegance
Cut slices of damson cheese into small shapes with biscuit cutters
and place round the apple. The contrast of colour and taste is very
effective.

DANISH APPLE CHARLOTTE

SERVES FIVE TO SIX

1 kg/2 lb apples
1 lemon
¼ litre/½ pint coarse fresh
  breadcrumbs

75 g/3 oz sugar
125 g/4 oz butter
icing sugar
approx. 225 g/½ lb raspberry jam

Peel, core and slice the apples. Put the sugar, 60 g (2 oz) butter,
grated lemon rind and the lemon juice into a pan with the apples;
stew gently until soft. If necessary raise the heat to reduce moisture
as the purée should be fairly dry. Set on one side.

Fry breadcrumbs in the remaining butter until golden brown
and crisp. Cover the base of a glass bowl with a thin layer of jam.
Spread the jam with half the apple purée and add another thin
layer of jam and half the crumbs. Repeat layers, finishing with

crumbs. Sift icing sugar over top.
Serve well chilled with pouring cream.

APPLE IDEAS

Most years a good apple harvest ensures that in the country at least they are abundant. It is quick and easy to transform windfalls or hedgerow pickings into tempting dishes.

Add chopped crystallized ginger and a little of the syrup to sweetened apple purée. Top with chopped nuts.

Poach peeled, cored apple slices in any mulled wine, punch or cider cup left over from Christmas parties. Sweeten to taste.

To create *Apple Snow*, whisk 3 egg whites until stiff and fold in 225 g (½ lb) apple purée flavoured with grated lemon rind.

Sweeten and flavour cooked apple purée with several tablespoons of coarse cut marmalade.

APPLE CRISP

SERVES FOUR TO SIX

1 kg/2 lb cooking apples   *50 g/2 oz sugar*

For the topping
  175 g/6 oz porridge oats   *125 g/4 oz butter*
  175 g/6 oz soft brown sugar   *½ teaspoon cinnamon*
  175 g/6 oz flour

Peel, core and slice the apples into a shallow ovenproof dish; sprinkle with sugar and 2 tablespoons water. Cut the butter into small pieces and rub in the flour. Mix in all the remaining ingredients and spread evenly over the apples. Press down lightly and bake at 375° F (190° C or Gas no. 5) for 40 minutes.
  Serve with egg custard.

DAMSON KISSEL

SERVES SIX

450 g/1 lb damsons
175 g/6 oz sugar
2 tablespoons potato flour

425 ml/¾ pint water
150 ml/¼ pint elderberry wine

Remove any stalks from the fruit and put in a saucepan with water. Bring to the boil and simmer for approximately 15 minutes. Sieve and return to a clean pan. Add the sugar and stir until dissolved. Mix the potato flour with the wine and blend into the hot fruit juice. Stir over a low heat until the purée thickens and clears. Pour into a glass serving bowl. When set spike with blanched almonds.

Serve very cold with cream handed separately.

DAMSON ICE CREAM

SERVES SIX TO EIGHT

1 kg/2 lb damsons
¼ litre/½ pint whipping cream

275 g/10 oz sugar

Wash the damsons and remove any stalks. Put in a saucepan with minimum amount of water to cover base and simmer covered until the fruit is cooked. Sieve and add sugar to taste, stir to dissolve and set aside to cool. Chill.

Whip cream into soft peaks and fold into the chilled fruit purée. Pour into an ice cube tray or lidded container for the freezer and leave until the edges start to freeze. Empty the ice cream into a chilled bowl and beat with an egg whisk until smooth and creamy. Return to freezer.

Two hours before the meal, place the ice cream in the refrigerator; the consistency when eaten should be firm and smooth but not rock hard.

Damsons freeze exceptionally well and it is worth making a

quantity of the purée for use during the year in fools, mousses and ice cream.

DAMSON CLAFOUTIS

SERVES FOUR

450 g/1 lb damsons
3 tablespoons flour
¼ litre/½ pint milk
50 g/2 oz butter

3 eggs
3 tablespoons castor sugar
150 ml/¼ pint single cream
pinch salt

Remove any stalks from the damsons and lay them in a shallow, well-greased oven dish.

Make a rich batter by adding the flour and salt to the beaten eggs. Stir in the sugar and beat until pale and thick. Add the warmed milk and cream and beat thoroughly together. Pour over the damsons. Dot with butter and bake at 375° F, 190° C or Gas no. 5) for 35 minutes until well risen and golden.

The batter sinks a little after being taken from the oven. Sprinkle castor sugar generously over the top and follow the French habit of serving the Clafoutis lukewarm, though it is equally delicious hot or cold.

This is an adaptation of the popular French recipe in which black cherries are used.

SUMMER PUDDING (2)

SERVES SIX TO EIGHT

1 kg/2 lb damsons or mixture
of apples and damsons

175 ml/1 gill water

Simmer the damsons until tender. Remove the stones and continue as for recipe given on page 58 for raspberry Summer Pudding. Allow approximately 125 g (4 oz) extra sugar when using damsons.

OATEN DAMSON PUDDING

SERVES FOUR

450 g/1 lb damsons
125 g/4 oz coarse oatmeal
2 eggs

125 g/4 oz sugar
½ litre/1 pint milk

Butter a deep pie dish. Heat the milk to boiling and pour over the oatmeal and sugar. Leave for at least an hour. Stone the damsons and stir with the beaten eggs into the oatmeal mixture. Bake in preheated moderate oven (350° F, 180° C or Gas no. 4) for 1 hour.

COUNTRY APPLE CAKE

450 g/1 lb cooking apples
25 g/1 oz butter
2 tablespoons lemon juice
175 g/6 oz raisins
50 g/2 oz shelled walnuts
175 g/6 oz currants
175 g/6 oz margarine

275 g/10 oz plain flour
1½ teaspoons bicarbonate of soda
2 tablespoons golden syrup
1 teaspoon ground ginger
½ teaspoon ground cinnamon
2 eggs
pinch of salt

Peel, core and chop the apples. Cook with the lemon juice and butter over a low heat until quite soft. Beat to a purée and leave until cold.

Line a 20-cm (8-inch) diameter cake tin with double thickness greaseproof paper.

Mix the flour, salt, bicarbonate of soda and spices; sift twice. Chop the walnuts and add to the dried fruit.

Cream the fat, syrup and sugar. When light, add the eggs, one at time. Stir the flour mixture into the eggs lightly, alternating with the apple purée. Add the fruit and nuts.

Turn into the prepared tin and make a deep hollow in the centre. Bake on the middle shelf of a preheated oven (325° F, 170° C or Gas no. 3) for at least 2 hours or until firm and brown.

Leave the cake to cool for ½ hour before turning out, and leave until quite cold before removing the paper.

Store for 1 week before cutting.

FRENCH APPLE GINGERBREAD

This is one of the most popular items on sale in the Champs Elysées on public holidays.

225 g/½ lb cooking apples	*225 g/½ lb self-raising flour*
125 g/4 oz butter	*1 egg*
125 g/4 oz soft brown sugar	*1 teaspoon ground ginger*
25 g/1 oz chopped candied peel	*½ teaspoon caraway seeds (optional)*

Grease and line a 1 kg (2 lb) loaf tin. Roughly chop the apples and simmer in minimum water until soft. Sieve and sweeten the purée. Set aside until cold.

Melt the butter and brown sugar together; cool and add a beaten egg. Sift the flour and ginger together into large bowl. Stir in the melted butter mixture, the apple purée, candied peel and caraway seeds if used. Beat these all together and pour into the prepared tin.

Bake in a pre-heated oven (325° F, 170° C or Gas no. 3) for about 50 minutes or until rich golden brown.

This lightly spiced cake is excellent for picnics and remains deliciously moist.

For special occasions add the following topping, *fudge frosting*:

50/2 oz butter	*2 tablespoons water*
175 g/6 oz sifted icing sugar	*vanilla essence*

Melt the butter with the water over a moderate heat; do not allow to boil. Remove from the heat and beat in the sifted icing sugar. Flavour with vanilla essence. Cool a little and beat again before spreading over the gingerbread.

APPLE GINGER CONSERVE

1½ kg/3 lb cooking apples
1 tablespoon lemon juice in
   275 ml/½ pint water
2 lemons

1½ kg/3 lb sugar
25 g/1 oz root ginger
125 g/¼ lb crystallized ginger
275 ml/½ pint water

Peel and core the apples, and slice into water and lemon juice to prevent discoloration.

Place the peel and cores in a saucepan with 275 ml (½ pint) water; simmer for 15 minutes. Bruise the ginger and tie in muslin with the thinly peeled rind from the lemons. Drain the apple slices and put them in a preserving pan with the strained water from the peel, muslin bag and sugar. Heat very gently until the sugar is dissolved. Cook until the apple slices are transparent and the conserve has reached setting point. Remove the muslin bag.

Stir in the chopped crystallized ginger. Pot and seal as for jam.

Made up in small pots, this unusual conserve makes a welcome present. Use as a filling for flans and pancakes, with ice cream or just enjoy a spoonful on its own, as it would be served abroad.

APPLE GINGER JAM

If jam consistency is wanted, follow the recipe above but stir the mixture vigorously while the sugar is dissolving. This will reduce the apple slices to the more usual purée.

APPLE CHEESE

2 kg/4 lb apples
brown sugar
½ teaspoon salt

1½ litres/3 pints cider
1 teaspoon each powdered cloves,
   cinnamon, allspice

Boil the cider in an open pan until reduced by half. Add washed and chopped apples; do not core or peel. Cover and simmer over a low heat until tender. Sieve.

Weigh the purée and add 450 g (1 lb) sugar to every ½ litre (1 pint) of apple. Add the spices and salt and cook over a very low heat, stirring continuously. When all the surplus liquid has been absorbed and the cheese is thick and rich brown in colour, pour into warmed jars and seal.

If straight-sided jars are available, the cheese can be turned out for slicing for a dessert.

Allow to mature for 4–6 weeks before using.

With their high proportion of sugar to fruit, cheeses have a similar shelf life to jam. As the name implies, a fruit cheese is sufficiently solid to slice, whereas fruit butter has a soft spreading consistency.

SPICED CRAB APPLES

1½ kg/3 lb crab apples　　*piece root ginger, cinnamon stick,*
½ kg/1 lb sugar　　　　　　*3 cloves, 6 peppercorns*
strip lemon peel　　　　　　*½ litre/1 pint cider vinegar*

Select apples which are only just ripe to ensure they remain whole. Put the spices and lemon in a muslin bag and place with the sugar and vinegar in a saucepan. Bring to the boil and add the apples and lemon peel. Cover and simmer on a very low heat until just tender. Leave the fruit in the syrup overnight.

Next day remove the apples with a perforated spoon and put them into jars. A few small pieces of root ginger can be inserted among the apples for extra flavour if liked.

Strain the liquid into a clean saucepan and boil rapidly for 10–15 minutes to reduce to the consistency of syrup. Cover the fruit with the hot syrup and seal with synthetic skin.

Keep for 6 weeks before using.

A jar of spiced crab apples makes an excellent present and the fruit is delicious served with the traditional rich Christmas goose or pork.

CRAB APPLE JELLY

2 kg/4 lb sound crab apples   *1 litre/2 pints water*
1 lemon   *sugar*

Put the washed fruit and lemon rind into a preserving pan with water; simmer to a pulp. Pour into a jelly bag and leave to drain.

Do not crush or press fruit as this will spoil the clarity of the final jelly.

Measure the juice and allow ½ kg (1 lb) sugar to each ½ litre (1 pint). Reheat the juice, adding the warmed sugar. Boil rapidly until setting point is reached and pour into warmed jars.

Cover and seal as usual.

PLUM PICKLE

2 kg/4 lb bullace or damsons   *1 kg/2 lb demerara sugar*
½ litre/1 pint vinegar   *1 tablespoon pickling spice*

Choose large, even-sized fruit and pack into kilner jars. Place in a moderate oven and cook until the skins begin to split. This method avoids unnecessary handling of the fruit and helps to ensure it remains whole.

Boil together the vinegar, sugar and pickling spice for 10 minutes. For extra flavour place a 3-cm (1-inch) cinnamon stick and 2 cloves in each jar. Strain the hot syrup over the fruit.

Cover when cold and keep for 2 months before using.

APPLE AND DAMSON BUTTER

1½ kg/3 lb apples   *½ kg/1 lb damsons*
sugar

Wipe over the fruit and remove any stalks or bruises. Roughly chop the apples and place in a large pan with the damsons and minimum water to cover the base. Cover and cook slowly until tender. Sieve the fruit, pushing through as much pulp as possible.

Weigh and return to the pan adding 350 g (¾ lb) sugar for each ½ kg (1 lb) of pulp. Stir until the sugar is dissolved. Continue stirring until the fruit is thick and of a spreading butter consistency.

Fruit butters should be made in small quantities for short term use. They are delicious spread on bread or toast instead of jam or served with cream cheese as a dessert.

DAMSON AND PORT SAUCE

225 g/½ lb wild plums
2 cloves
3 cm (1 inch) stick cinnamon
2 tablespoons soft brown
  sugar

½ pint elderberry wine or port
2 oranges
1 lemon
2 tablespoons bramble jelly

Place fruit, wine, cloves and cinnamon in a saucepan and simmer until soft. Remove the spices and sieve, extracting as much purée as possible. Reheat with the jelly, sugar, grated rind and juice of the oranges and lemon. Mix well and taste for seasoning.

Use hot with braised tongue or venison.

SLOE AND APPLE JELLY

½ kg/1 lb sloes (picked
  after first frost)
sugar

½ kg/1 lb apples
¼ litre/½ pint water

Pick over the fruit, removing any stalks. Roughly chop the apples and put in a preserving pan with the sloes and water. Cover and simmer until soft. Strain through a jelly bag overnight.

Measure the juice and allow ½ kg (1 lb) sugar to each ½ litre (1 pint). Stir the sugar into the juice and bring to the boil. Boil rapidly until setting point is reached and pour into small jars.

This jelly has a lovely colour and should be served with cold meats or game.

DAMSON CHEESE

damsons   *sugar*

Clean the fruit and put into a heavy pan. Add water to barely cover. Simmer with the lid on over a gentle heat until the fruit is thoroughly cooked. Rub the pulp through a sieve. Crack a few of the stones and add the kernels to the pulp. Weigh the pulp and add an equal amount of sugar. Stir in the sugar and continue cooking, stirring regularly until a spoon cut across the mixture leaves a firm line—after about 1–1¾ hours. Pour the cheese into small straight-sided pots and cover as for jam.

Before the arrival of the deep freeze, every country housewife had a larder filled with preserves. Fruit cheeses are an excellent winter standby; they should be kept for several months until crystallized on top.

Turn out and serve sliced with cream, to accompany apple dishes or with cream cheese and biscuits.

BULLACE RELISH

MAKES 3 KG/7 LB

1½ kg/3 lb bullace   *½ kg/1 lb apples*
½ kg/1 lb onions   *225 g/8 oz carrots*
½ kg/1 lb brown sugar   *½ litre/1 pint cider vinegar*
125 g/4 oz salt   *½ kg/1 lb raisins*
1 teaspoon each of ground cloves, cinnamon, ground ginger and nutmeg

Stone the fruit; slice and chop the onions, apples and carrots. Add the plums and raisins and put all through a mincer. Place the fruit mixture in half the vinegar and simmer for about 45 minutes until soft.

Boil the remaining vinegar with sugar, salt and spices for about 10 minutes and strain into the fruit. Continue cooking, stirring occasionally until all the liquid is absorbed and the relish is of a thick, sauce-like consistency, about 1–1½ hours.

Pour into clean warm bottles and tie down with plastic skin immediately.

APPLE CHUTNEY

Chutneys are probably the most flexible form of cookery as exact quantities are unimportant. Experiment with a mixture of available fruits and spices. Like wine, all chutneys improve if allowed to mature. Apple chutney is one of the most popular; here are two examples from either end of the taste spectrum.

SWEET APPLE CHUTNEY

MAKES 2 KG/4 LB

½ kg/1 lb apples
225 g/8 oz raisins
350 g/12 oz brown sugar
25 g/1 oz salt
½ litre/1¼ pints vinegar

225 g/8 oz onions
125 g/4 oz preserved ginger
2 bananas
½ teaspoon ground mixed spice
275 ml/½ pint water

Put the peeled apples, bananas and onions through the mincer and place in a saucepan. Add the raisins and the chopped ginger. Simmer in 275 ml (½ pint) water with the saucepan covered until tender, approximately ¾ hour.

Add the vinegar, spice, sugar and salt and continue cooking in an uncovered pan until thick. Ladle into clean hot jars and tie down immediately with synthetic skin.

Keep for 3 months before use.

HOT INDIAN APPLE CHUTNEY

2 kg/4 lb apples	*1 kg/2 lb raisins*
2 kg/4 lb brown sugar	*225 g/½ lb salt*
2 cloves garlic	*50 g/2 oz red chillies*
125 g/4 oz mustard seed	*25 g/1 oz ground ginger*
1 litre/2 pints vinegar	*10 g/½ oz allspice*

Peel, core and slice the apples and simmer them in 1 pint vinegar until tender. Mince the raisins and chillies; crush the garlic with a little salt.

Dissolve the sugar in the second pint of vinegar and boil to reduce to a light syrup. Add the remaining ingredients and place covered in a slow oven for 3–4 hours until all the liquid is absorbed and the chutney is thick.

Bottle while hot and seal with synthetic skin.

Keep for 6 months and use with caution!

The yield of chutney recipes will vary according to the time and speed at which the ingredients are cooked.

APPLE WINE

MAKES SIX BOTTLES

3 kg/6 lb apples, including up to 1 kg/2 lb crab apples if possible

250 g/8 oz raisins	*4½ litres/1 gallon water*
25 g/1 oz wine yeast	*1 tablespoon yeast nutrient*
1¼ kg/2½ lb sugar	*1 lemon*

Chop or crush the apples. A quick short cut to this process can be made by putting the apples in a polythene bag in the deep freeze for 48 hours. Remove and thaw; they will be soft enough to crush with the hands.

Place the apple pulp in an earthenware or plastic container and add the chopped raisins, thinly peeled lemon rind and sugar. Pour on boiling water. Stir well and cover. When cooled to 21° C (70° F) add lemon juice, yeast and nutrient.

Keep closely covered in a warm place and stir well every day for a week. Strain into storage jar and fit airlock. Leave to continue fermentation for 3 months; siphon into clean jars; repeat after another two months and if wine is clear, siphon into bottles and cork.

Keep for a year before use.

APPLE ALE

FILLS FOUR QUART BOTTLES

1 kg/2 lb apples	*¾ kg/1½ lb sugar*
2 litres/1 gallon water	*½ teaspoon cinnamon*
2 pieces of root ginger	*½ teaspoon ground cloves*

Mince or grate the apples coarsely and place all the pulp and cores into a large container with the water. Stir well and cover. Stir daily for one week and then strain. Add all the remaining ingredients; stir and leave for 24 hours. Strain into bottles.

Cork and leave for 7 days before drinking.

LAMBS WOOL

1 kg/2 lb crab apples	*1 litre/1 quart Old Ale*
soft brown sugar	*(Ruddles or Old Country)*
1 stick cinnamon	*½ teaspoon each freshly grated*
	nutmeg and ground ginger

Roast the apples until soft and sieve them. Warm the ale with the spices and set aside to infuse for 10 minutes. Remove the cinnamon stick and pour the liquid over the apple purée. Sweeten to taste and return to the saucepan to reheat. Do not allow to boil.

Drink warm.

SLOE GIN

*sloes (picked after the   castor sugar
first frost)   gin*

Select sound fruit, remove the stalks and prick each one several times with a large needle or skewer. Pack into wide necked bottles. Add sugar and fill to the top with gin.

Proportions for a standard glass fruit juice bottle are: 350 g (¾ lb) fruit, 175 g (6 oz) sugar and ¾ bottle gin.

Cork securely and keep in a warm, frequented position in order to shake the bottle every day or so until the sugar is dissolved. After 3 months strain through double muslin and bottle. It will keep indefinitely and improves with age.

The drained fruit should be put in an airtight jar. Consumption of the berries is really the cook's perk but a few added to an apple pie give an excellent flavour.

BULLACE WINE

MAKES SIX BOTTLES

*2 kg/4 lb bullaces   250 g/8 oz raisins
1½ kg/3 lb sugar   4½ litres/1 gallon water
25 g/1 oz wine yeast   1 tablespoon pectic enzyme
25 g/1 oz yeast nutrient*

Stalk the bullaces and wash them thoroughly in very hot water containing a little washing soda in order to remove the waxy bloom. Rinse the fruit and place in a fermenting bucket. Pour over boiling water. When cool, add the pectic enzyme, stir well and cover. Leave for 24 hours before adding yeast and nutrient.

Cover and leave for 4 days, stirring daily. Strain onto the sugar and keep covered in a warm place for a week. Pour into a fermenting jar, fit the air-lock and ferment. Siphon into clean jars when the wine is clear and leave to mature for 6 months before bottling. Serve as a table wine.

NOTES

BIBLIOGRAPHY

Addy, S. O., *Folk Tales and Superstitions*, 1895, reprint 1973

Bates, Margaret, *Talking About Cakes*, Pergamon Press, 1964

Berry, C. J. J., *First Steps in Winemaking*, Amateur Winemaker Publications, 1976

Bullock, H. D. McCully, H. and Noderer, E., *The American Heritage Cookbook*, Penguin, 1967

Evans, George Ewart, *The Pattern Under the Plough*, Faber, 1966

Farmhouse Fare, Farmers Weekly

Graves, Robert, *The White Goddess*, Faber, 1952

Grieve, M., *A Modern Herbal*, Jonathan Cape, 1931

Grigson, Geoffrey, *The Englishman's Flora*, Phoenix House, 1958

Grigson, Jane, *English Food*, Macmillan, 1974 and *The Mushroom Feast*, Michael Joseph, 1975

Heath, Ambrose, *Good Soups*, Faber, 1935 and *Good Puddings and Pies*, Faber 1947

Hedges and Local History, National Council of Social Service, 1971

Hemphill, Rosemary, *Herbs and Spices*, Penguin, 1966

Hole, Christina, *British Folk Customs*, Hutchinson, 1976

Hume, Rosemary and Downes, Muriel, *Jams, Preserves and Pickles*, Chatto and Windus, 1960

Jacob, Dorothy, *A Witch's Guide to Gardening*, Elek Books, 1964

James, B., *Wild Fruits, Berries, Nuts & Flowers*, Medici Society, 1942

Mabey, Richard, *Food for Free*, Collins, 1972

Nilson, Bee (Ed), *The WI Diamond Jubilee Cookbook*, Heinemann, 1975

Petrova, Nina, *Russian Cookery*, Penguin, 1968

Ramsbottom, John, *Edible Fungi*, King Penguin, 1943

Sarson, Henry, *Home Pickling*, C. Arthur Pearson Ltd, rev. ed. 1949

Spry, Constance and Hume, Rosemary, *The Constance Spry Cookery Book*, Dent, 1956

Westland, Pamela, *A Taste of the Country*, Penguin, 1976

Young, Andrew, *A Prospect of Flowers*, Jonathan Cape, 1945

and many bulging volumes of cookery scrap books filled with anonymous cuttings and recipes from family and friends; for any of those used but not acknowledged I apologize but offer deep gratitude for the pleasure the recipe has given.

INDEX